TRANSFORMING PROBLEMS

Transforming Problems

Bert Ghezzi

SERVANT BOOKS
Ann Arbor, Michigan

Copyright © 1986 by Bert Ghezzi
All rights reserved
Published by Servant Books
P.O. Box 8617
Ann Arbor, Michigan 48107
86 87 88 89 90 91 10 9 8 7 6 5 4 3 2 1
Printed in the United States of America
ISBN 0-89283-294-0

Library of Congress Cataloging in Publication Data

Ghezzi, Bert.
  Transforming problems.

  1. Christian life—1960—   . I. Title.
BV4501.2.G475 1986   248.4   85-30389
ISBN 0-89283-294-0

Table of Contents

1. Turning Points / 7
2. Guilt / 15
3. Turning from Sin / 23
4. Disappointment / 33
5. Turning to God in Surrender / 39
6. Lust and Other Disorderly Desires / 49
7. Turning to God's Love / 57
8. Loneliness / 67
9. Turning to Others through Love / 75
10. Low Self-Esteem / 83
11. Forgiveness, Service, and Encouragement / 91
12. Worry / 97
13. Turning to God in Faith / 105
14. Becoming More Like Jesus / 113

ONE

Turning Points

WHEN I FIRST BEGAN to follow the Lord seriously, the Christian life was a snap. Perhaps your experience has been the same. Things sailed along. The Lord seemed very present to me. My efforts to serve him seemed very productive. Problems which had plagued me through my teen years and early twenties faded into the background. Yes, the Christian life was good, and it seemed so easy.

The picture soon changed. Within months of my making an adult decision to follow Jesus, some of the old problems began to crop up again. They even seemed to be a little stickier. To my surprise they also stayed around. New problems raised their ugly heads, and some of them seemed worse than any I had gone through previously.

"What on earth is going on?" I asked an older and wiser Christian friend.

"Do you know what happens when you pour clean water into a dirty bucket?" he asked. Then, as older and wiser friends tend to do, he answered his own question.

"Well, all that surface dirt floods to the top. Then the scum you didn't know was there gets flushed out too. You can either stand there and complain, 'what a filthy bucket!' or you can be glad for the chance to clean it up."

I didn't like being compared to a scummy bucket, but I got the point. When you become a committed follower of Jesus, the Holy Spirit is at work cleaning you up, so problems begin to surface in order to be dealt with. The difference is that Jesus is setting the agenda now instead of you. Some things emerge that you used to ignore or failed to see but which he wants to work on.

The longer I live the Christian life, the more I am convinced of the truth of this principle. I suggest we formulate it as a Christian corollary to Murphy's Law. We could state it this way: the more serious we become about being a Christian, the more problems the Lord allows us to have for our own good. This corollary would be called "The Peter and Paul Principle," after the two great apostles who grew in faith and faced numerous troubles until they died as martyrs.

Problems as Opportunities

A retired admiral taught me the value of problems in the Christian life. He gave the main address at a friend's graduation, and he spoke about courage. He explained that he was widely known and respected for his bravery, a reputation he had won in combat. He said that when bombs were bursting in air over the ship, he would become more obviously deliberate in all his speech and actions. His men read this as courage, and it was. "I was really scared as hell," the admiral said, "but I knew that if I acted courageously, the men would too."

The admiral had grasped, perhaps unwittingly, one of the paradoxical secrets of Christian living. A problem can be the occasion for our destruction or a chance for our strengthening. The admiral's fear could have immobilized him, costing many lives and winning for him the reputation of cowardice. Instead, fear made him act courageously, and it can be said to be the cause of the virtue which won him respect.

This is true for other problems. For example, rage, which has more than enough raw energy to destroy us, can dispose us to holiness. It is a prerequisite for patience, just as discouragement is for hope.

Courage would be a pretty tame thing without fear to motivate it, don't you think? Chastity would be as bland as baby cereal were there no sexual temptations for it to subdue. I even doubt that Christian qualities like kindness can exist at all without something like meanness to call them out of us.

Seen this way, our problems can be advantages instead of disasters. When we are living as disciples of Christ, our difficulties become opportunities for growth. They are occasions which enable God to transform us so that we become more like Jesus.

Risk and Ruin

This positive view of personal problems ought not gull us into thinking that they are nice and that their story will always end with everyone living happily ever after. That would be as naive as those modern revisions of the tale of Little Red Riding Hood, in which the wolf does not really eat the girl.

For example, disorderly desires are not petty problems, the sort that we might simply grow out of. Lust, greed, envy, hatred and the like are dangerous, for they have the power to ruin us. Recently, I read about a Christian pastor who asked another pastor to help him break an addiction to pornography. The second pastor broke down weeping, confessing to his friend his own long-standing problem with sexual sin. Lust had instigated his demise: he had contracted a venereal disease; his wife of twenty-five years was divorcing him; his children were alienated from him; his church was scandalized and his ministry ruined.

Why does the Lord allow such bad things to happen to good people? How can his love tolerate our degradation? We can guess, but we can never know with certainty. Perhaps humiliation is the Lord's last resort in convincing obstinate people to receive his mercy.

How many times on a downward spiral do we glimpse the Lord's hand offering rescue, and refuse to take hold? God permits us to flirt with mortal danger, until at last we have nowhere to turn but to him. There is the risk that we may never surrender to God, and then we are lost. However, there is hope even for the most desperate cases, for as potent as our personal problems may be, they cannot extinguish the fire of God's love.

Turning Points

Our problems can be turning points for us. A turning point is a point at which something changes direction, or a point at which a decisive change occurs. A problem can propel us in an evil direction, or it can move us toward the good. The presupposition of this book is hopeful, expecting readers to perceive problems as potential benefits and to allow themselves to be drawn by them nearer to God.

The concept of a turning point, a decisive change of direction, is dynamic. The very words "turning," "change," and "direction" imply movement and suggest a source of energy. When we are having a problem, there seems to be a spiritual law of gravity at work, dragging us almost inevitably to an evil destination—sin, ruin, desperation, or you name it. Where does the impetus to break this spiritual inertia come from?

If we were to answer this question by observing Christians who were trying to wriggle free from the weight of personal problems, we would have to say most of us behave as though we had the power to conquer them ourselves. However, in rational moments or in fits of truthful exasperation, we confess that we can't handle it. We haven't got the personal spiritual energy to create our own turning points.

The only power capable of turning a problem to our advantage is the love of God. One of the goals of this book is to persuade readers to align their behavior with this truth. Paul had this to say about the dynamism of God's love:

> We rejoice in our sufferings, knowing that suffering produces endurance, and endurance produces character, and character produces hope, and hope does not disappoint us, because God's love has been poured into our hearts through the Holy Spirit which has been given to us. (Rom 5:3-5)

God allows us to suffer so that he can bring us to pivotal places where we can turn away from evil and turn toward him. His love puts us on the spot and brings us to our turning points.

This is a book about how the love of God works persistently to free us from personal problems. Six common problems have been selected to illustrate how the Lord uses difficulties to refashion us in Christ's image.

Getting free of big personal problems may involve

complex changes for us, but almost always we must turn from sin, turn to God, and turn toward others by loving them more. The six problems discussed were chosen because they illustrate various ways in which difficulties can be opportunities for Christian growth. Thus each chapter about a problem is immediately followed by one which shows how it can be a turning point, bringing us benefit instead of loss.

Here is a list of the chapters about problems paired with their companion chapters showing the turning points:

2. Guilt
3. Turning from Sin: We can resolve our difficulties with guilt and guilt feelings by breaking with our sinfulness and giving our heart afresh to God.

4. Disappointment
5. Turning to God in Surrender: The cure for disappointment is a heartfelt decision to accept the circumstances of life on God's terms.

6. Lust and Other Disorderly Desires
7. Turning to God in Love: The love of God can burn so brightly in us that it will replace the lesser stars of our unruly desires.

8. Loneliness
9. Turning to Others through Love: Expressing love for others is an antidote for loneliness.

10. Low Self-Esteem
11. Forgiveness, Service, and Encouragement: The best way to learn self-love is to lose yourself in loving others.

12. Worry
13. Turning to God in Faith: Even worry can have a good result if it occasions our growing in faith.

If we will see our problems with spiritual eyes, we will be able to approach them as chances to become mature followers of Christ. Seen as turning points, they can leave us stronger and better Christians instead of simply damaging us or even doing us in.

TWO

Guilt

MAGAZINES SOMETIMES SELL a gift subscription by telling us it is a "gift that keeps on giving" because it keeps coming back every week. However, one of America's best homespun philosophers, Erma Bombeck, says that the real gift that keeps on giving is guilt.

Guilt and its by-product, guilt feelings, are problems of epidemic proportions in our society. Here are some representative examples:

Ten years ago, when Molly was sixteen, she had an abortion. Panic and pressure from Mark, her boyfriend, had pushed her to do it. Molly had been confused, feeling deeply that she was murdering her baby, yet simultaneously wanting to believe that she was simply eliminating a glob of fetal tissue. She can still remember the searing pain of the injection. Worse, the realization—no longer clouded by confusion—that she killed the child in her womb convulses her with anguish. A heavy deposit of guilt still depresses Molly's spirit.

Tom is a certified public accountant for a "Big Eight" firm. Once his work buddies were treating a client to an evening at a topless bar and invited him along. Advertisements for adult entertainment centers tantalized Tom, but he had always fought off their enticements. However, this time his curiosity bettered him. He told his wife Jean, who was used to an accountant's erratic hours, that he had to work late. So, Tom tagged along for the fun. It turned out to be a night of "firsts" for Tom—his first time at a topless bar; the first time he got drunk; the first time he toyed with the idea of adultery; and the first time he lied to Jean. Now Tom feels like he betrayed his wife. He is afraid she might find out about his little escapade. When he recalls how much he enjoyed his flirtation with lust, he feels even more guilty.

Bill has a serious problem with anger, which is aggravated by the pressures of his life. He is an assistant manager at a discount department store; he takes classes towards his M.B.A. two weekday nights; he and his wife Mary have three children, ages six, four, and one. Bill has enough willpower to confine his outbursts to home. There his pent up rage explodes. Hardly a week goes by when he has not spanked one of the children furiously and without cause. Twice in three years he has slapped Mary. Bill wants to be a good husband and father and is very ashamed of his angry behavior. He is plagued by guilt but cannot seem to stop lashing out at his family.

There are many like Molly, Tom, and Bill, whose difficulties are compounded by nagging guilt. There are numerous others who say they do not feel guilty, even when they have abortions, indulge in lust, or beat their children. They have mistaken the feeling of guilt with its objective presence. They are affected by it without knowing it, as we shall see in the next chapter. There is the hope that someday they may wake up appreciating guilt, like the very proper elderly lady in the *New Yorker* cartoon, who, reclining on the couch, tells her psychiatrist, "I just want my inhibitions back."

The Mae West Theory of Personal Morality

The pop-psychology industry has made many of today's gurus rich by taking advantage of our desire to ease the emotional pain caused by guilt feelings. In their offices and in the media, counselors tell us that the way to deal with guilt is either to ignore it or to get around it. They advise us to make ourselves comfortable with behavior that makes us feel guilty. We will feel a lot better, they say, if we tune out our conscience, or at least re-set it according to modern rather than medieval standards.

At every turn, we are urged to shed outmoded views of sin and to decide what is right or wrong for ourselves on the basis of how we feel about it. A local radio station, for example, has been broadcasting a public service announcement aimed at persuading teens to break with the crowd by abstaining from drugs and alcohol. This is a well-intentioned effort, except that the young man making the appeal says that he wants to live responsibly because, "I like me, and I want to live out how *I* feel." That's fine for now, while he wants to avoid getting high. However, what happens to his personal standard of morality when he feels like indulging himself a little?

Commonly, pop-psychology vendors tell us that the imposition of external standards over our feelings acts as a major source of guilt. For example, our local newspaper used to feature a weekly advice column for teenagers. Once a sixteen-year-old boy wrote in for help because he was ashamed of having enjoyed sex with another boy. He was told that since he felt he had done something "wrong" he must sort out his "confusion between his own personal feelings and outside messages [he] may be reacting to." His parents, school, friends, church, and, yes, alas, even television, may be forcing rules on him that mess up his feelings.

I call this approach "The Mae West Theory of Personal Morality" because of its kinship with West's popular axiom, "To err is human, but it feels divine." In a nutshell, we are advised to consult our feelings, not any external standards or authorities, to determine what is good or bad for us. Parents, pastors, and other authority figures are not in touch with how we feel and do not want to be. They merely set arbitrary limits which restrict our behavior and make us unhappy. We are exhorted to assert ourselves over the standards; to refuse to listen to outside authorities; and to repeat guilt-inducing behavior until we feel okay about it.

Common Dodges

We should not be surprised at the popularity of the advice, since it fits right in with the familiar dodges people have always used in efforts to avoid paying the price of wrongdoing. We try to bypass the pain of guilt by pretending that what we have done is not wrong or by making excuses which eliminate our responsibility for the offending behavior.

Cover-ups. A common way of fooling ourselves is accomplished by choosing nice, attractive names for our sins in preference to the nastier, more accurate names. Several years ago, for example, a writer hyped the film *The Blue Lagoon* as an excellent way to introduce adolescents to an "authentic, mature love relationship." However, a reviewer in *The New Yorker* said the film was nothing more than a showcase for two teenage sex idols, a fishbowl for their skinny-dipping until they inevitably discovered "fornication."

We have invented a dictionary full of lovely terms to conceal sexual sin. People prefer to think they are involved in an authentic and mature love relationship. They never say that they are fornicating or committing adultery. Using those terms might shake them back to their senses.

The use of cosmetic language to disguise sin is widespread. We may know someone who is neurotically curious about the affairs of others. Instead of seeing himself as a busybody, he has persuaded himself he is expressing concern for others' welfare. He has convinced some others, too, for a few people even praise his meddling as an expression of Christian love. People who are so irritable that they cannot get along with others like to mark out their territory by spreading the positive word that they are "spunky" or "feisty." And we have all at one time or another mistakenly identified a withdrawn, depressed person as "humble" or a person without self-control in speech as "frank" or "candid."

Making Excuses. We adopt cover-ups because we hope to avoid guilt feelings by ignoring or reducing the seriousness of guilt-causing behavior. We also attempt to minimize guilt by insisting that we cannot be blamed for the offense. We work hard to whittle down our responsibility for some wrongful act, hoping that we may even be able to completely excuse ourselves. The following attempt of a father to sort out an argument between his sons illustrates the point:

DAD: Mark, did you hit Jim?
MARK: He called me a toad!
DAD: I didn't ask what Jim did. Did you hit him?
MARK: No, I didn't mean to hit him. I just wanted to scare him.
DAD: Did you strike him with your hand?
MARK: Not really. I might have touched him with my finger. I barely made contact with him at all!

All the while, Jim has been testifying that Mark indeed slugged him ("Look, I have a bruise where he hit me!") and excusing his own offensive name-calling by reporting that Mark had "spit in my milk."

Mark and Jim did not want to admit to anything until they had convinced their dad that they were not responsible for their actions. If they could not be blamed, so they reasoned, their fair-minded father would not punish them. Both boys denied culpability by claiming that something said or done by the other was enough provocation to clear them of responsibility. Neither believed he could be held accountable if he could show that the other "made me do it." Mark also invoked the classic excuse that he "didn't mean to do it."

The defense mechanisms Mark and Jim resorted to here are not the exclusive property of adolescents. We all try to dodge responsibility for wrongdoing by making excuses for ourselves. If we can find an excuse that eliminates, questions, or reduces our culpability, we then feel we can avoid guilt. We can become so preoccupied weighing the influence of provocation and sorting out motives that we lose sight of the fact that an offense has been committed. In extreme cases, we are like the lady in the cartoon who watched a shark wriggle over the beach to drag her husband to the sea, devouring him along the way. Reporting the tragedy to a policeman, the victim's hapless wife excused the shark by exclaiming, "Why, the poor thing must have been starved!"

The Truth About Guilt

At core, the popular advice and the familiar dodges are based on the same misunderstanding of guilt. They view it almost exclusively as a negative emotion with intense subjective force. Hence, they motivate us to construct elaborate internal devices to protect ourselves from its impact. Or they lead us to devise ways of getting around it.

It is a mistake to see guilt and guilt feelings as purely negative or destructive forces that must be eliminated. Guilt, like love and desire, is actually a positive force which motivates behavior that is essential to human society. For example, when we offend someone, guilt spurs us to repair the damage. Guilt should move Bill, who takes his anger out on his family, to ask his wife and children to forgive him. It may impel him to get the help he needs to subdue his rage. Guilt also may have the healthy effect of strengthening Tom's commitment to Jean, if it galvanizes his will to fight the allurements of lust.

Without guilt, human relationships would certainly deteriorate into an anarchy of selfishness, hatred, and crime. This point is demonstrated by those few among us who have no experience whatever of guilt. Psychologists correctly define their condition as a mental illness. They are called psychopaths. These people are able to commit heinous crimes without experiencing any remorse or guilt feelings. If all our misdirected efforts to eliminate guilt and guilt feelings were successful, the result would be more pain and unhappiness for everyone. The multitude that have already shed their inhibitions are exacting a high price from the rest of us.

The popular approaches to guilt are also mistaken in viewing it exclusively as an emotion. They confuse the most obvious part, the feelings which we experience very personally and intensively, with the whole of guilt, which is an objective condition due to some sinful deed. They end up applying superficial treatment to symptoms, like taking aspirin for a brain tumor or applying bandaids for dismemberment. They never deal with the reality of guilt. Thus they assure the grain of truth in Erma Bombeck's observation. Guilt just keeps on giving. Unless it is correctly dealt with.

THREE

Turning from Sin

THE REALITY OF SIN is the point which distinguishes the Christian view of guilt from contemporary misunderstandings. Christians confront the fact of sin. They do not attempt to pass over wrongdoing or to get around guilt, which are the fatal flaws of pop-psychology and the familiar dodges.

From Genesis to Revelation, the Bible consistently says that offenses against God must be paid for. The Old Testament taught Israel that sin was serious and punishment was due to the sinner. For example, Moses told the Israelites that if they obeyed all the commandments, the Lord would bless them in every way. But if Israel transgressed against God's laws, he would curse them. "Cursed shall you be in the city, and cursed shall you be in the field. Cursed shall be your basket and your kneading trough. Cursed shall be the fruit of your body, and the fruit of your ground, the increase of your cattle" (Dt 28:16-18). The message is unambiguous: grievous sin, grave consequences.

The New Testament continues this theme of reward or

punishment for our deeds. For example, consider this selection from the letter to the Romans, chapter 2, verses 5 to 11:

> But by your hard and impenitent heart you are storing up wrath for yourself on the day of wrath when God's righteous judgment will be revealed. For he will render to every man according to his works: to those who by patience in well-doing seek for glory and honor and immortality, he will give eternal life; but for those who are factious and do not obey the truth but obey wickedness, there will be wrath and fury.

Thus, God will reward holiness with eternal life and punish sin with eternal death, that is, separation from him forever.

According to the Old Testament, God demanded that sin be dealt with adequately. He allowed an atoning payment to be made for offenses, but it was costly. Atonement usually involved the shedding of animal blood, the offering of a life to pay for the sin. This foreshadowed the central event of the New Testament. Jesus Christ, the Son of God, became a man and offered his life—once for all—in a bloody sacrifice to atone for our sins.

A Sin Is a Sin

Current misunderstandings have so scrambled our perspective that we may have difficulty grasping the objectivity of sin. My own confusion on the subject vanished years ago because of a blatant traffic violation. I was driving 70 miles per hour, the posted speed limit, on a stretch of familiar country road, and I was occupying myself by taking a prayer time. I did not notice at all when the speed limit changed to 35 mph as the road began to pass through a little rural town.

I considered explaining to the policeman who pulled me over that my prayer had momentarily distracted my attention from my driving. It was something of an excuse. While it persuaded me that my reponsibility was reduced, it would not have counted much with the officer. He had hard evidence. His eyes and his radar agreed that I had been driving 70 mph in a 35 mph zone. I had sinned against the traffic laws and I had to pay for it. My excessive speed was an objective offense. My spiritual excuse did not alter its reality a bit.

Guilt Is Guilt

Guilt is the component of a sinful act that clamors for punishment. Have you noticed that when a distracted parent fails to discipline a naughty child, the child sometimes brazenly repeats the offensive act? The child's guiltiness demands a reckoning. It does not rest until the issue is settled. Children know intuitively that guilt hurts and that a spanking or its equivalent brings relief. Guilty adults demand punishment, too, but they express it in sophisticated forms, like self-defeating behavior. For example, if we have a violent argument with a friend and we are at fault, we may punish ourselves by avoiding other friends instead of quickly settling the offense.

Guilt is like a boulder challenging a stream. No matter how mighty the rushing waters, they cannot ignore the rock nor pretend that it isn't there. The stream crashes into the boulder, and with waves foaming and lashing wildly, it yields to reality and divides. To use another metaphor, guilt is like a powerful dye which when dumped in the stream stains every molecule of water. Not a drop remains that has not been tinged with its color. Guilt is an objective state. There's no denying it or evading it. No matter how hard we try. No matter how cleverly we reason. No matter how artfully we pretend.

The consequence of sin is guilt-that-will-not-quit, even for those among us who claim to be amoral. People who have dulled their consciences with repeated wrongdoing may be able to say truthfully that they don't feel very guilty, but that does not mean they are free of guilt. The Bible teaches that we accumulate guilt even when we sin unwittingly. The Old Testament, for example, told Israel how to offer atoning sacrifices for sins that people committed unintentionally (Lv 4, 5). Jesus himself said that the servant who did not know what the master wanted and therefore transgressed would still have to be punished (Lk 12:48). When Walter Hooper reported to C.S. Lewis a gravestone that read, "Here lies an atheist all dressed up with no place to go," Lewis commented wryly, "I bet he wishes that were true." In the end, guilt brings just punishment.

Unacknowledged guilt has inescapable side effects, like guilt feelings, which don't just go away on their own. People who don't feel guilty have very likely changed their guilt feelings into something else, usually something worse. For example, guilty people may push down the feelings that remind them of their evil behavior. Once suppressed, however, guilt feelings fester and may resurface disguised as irritability, depression, or self-pity.

Repentance and Responsibility

The only way to deal with guilt is to repent for the sin which produced it. This truth is woven into the very nature of things because it corresponds to the divine nature. When God revealed himself to Moses, he said he was "The Lord, a God merciful and gracious . . . forgiving iniquity and transgression and sin, but *who will by no means clear the guilty*" (Ex 34:6-7). God generously forgives those who turn to him in repentance. But those who remain adamant in their guilt he punishes justly. Mercy for the repentant, justice for the guilty.

The fundamental action in repentance involves taking responsibility for our wrongdoing. In order to be cleared of guilt, we must admit to ourselves and to God that we have done something wrong. For example, we must be able to say, "I spoke against him and ruined his reputation"; or "I was unfaithful to my spouse"; or "I embezzled $3,000 from my company"; and so on. There may be numerous circumstances which qualify our behavior and reduce our culpability. However, repentance involves an accurate assessment of what was done wrong and a simple admission of guilt. The Lord himself, the just judge, will weigh all the mitigating circumstances and set our punishment accordingly.

King David, Adulterer and Murderer

The story of David, the adulterer and murderer, is a case in point (2 Sm 11, 12). David seduced Bathsheba, the wife of Uriah the Hittite, who was one of his captains. When David found out that he had gotten Bathsheba pregnant, he tried to avoid responsibility for his sin. He arranged a temporary home leave from battle for Uriah, naturally expecting that he would sleep with his wife. However, since his men were at war and camping in the open, Uriah did not sleep with Bathsheba but stayed out of doors among David's servants. Unable to manipulate Uriah into covering up his adultery, David arranged for his murder. He instructed Joab, his commander, to put Uriah in the thick of the battle and draw back from him, so that he would be killed. Joab did exactly as the king commanded.

These grievous sins agonized David. "When I declared not my sin," he wrote later, "my body wasted away through my groaning all day long. For day and night thy hand was heavy upon me; my strength was dried up as by the heat of summer" (Ps 32:3-4). So David's guilt tortured him relentlessly.

The Lord sent Nathan to confront David. The prophet asked David's judgment about a rich man who had despoiled a poor man of his only ewe lamb, a case which stood for David's sins against Uriah. "The man who did this deserves to die," said David.

"You are the man," Nathan said. Then he set before David the facts about what he had done. David listened to Nathan and repented simply by saying, "I have sinned against the Lord." He later reflected on that moment of repentance in Psalm 32. "I acknowledged my sin to thee, and I did not hide my iniquity; I said, 'I will confess my transgressions to the Lord'; then thou didst forgive the guilt of my sin" (verse 5). David says he did not conceal his wickedness—he made no excuses nor protests about circumstances that might qualify his accountability. He accepted his responsibility for the sins and welcomed the punishment due to them. The Lord forgave him. He spared David's life, which by law his crimes had forfeited. However, David had to endure a reduced punishment. The child of the adulterous union died, and the Lord removed some of his protection from David's own family.

Ironically, the real way of getting around guilt takes exactly the opposite approach from the pop-psychological advice and the familiar defense mechanisms. The latter are based on efforts to eliminate guilt by shirking any personal responsibility for sin. Hence the assertion of personal feelings over moral standards, the cover-ups and pretenses, the avoidance of blame, and the invention of excuses are all at root mechanisms for shunning accountability for wrongdoing. Small wonder that those who use them experience guilt as the gift that keeps on giving.

Turning from Sin

Guilt is not something we want to live with. How are we to deal with it? Preventive medicine is most effective: to avoid guilt and guilt feelings, don't be guilty. Since, however, we are not perfect enough to always avoid sin, there is a simple biblical way to take care of guilt:

1. *Admit our sin to ourselves and to God.* All the factors which may have conditioned our behavior do not erase the fact of our sin. We did it. We must admit it and do something about it.

2. *Decide to turn away from the sin.* Repentance means having a change of heart. It involves a decision to stop our evil behavior and to avoid it in the future. To implement this choice, we will certainly have to take some practical steps to change our life to assure that we are able to follow through on it.

3. *Confess our sin to God and to anyone we may have harmed.* Telling God we are sorry for having offended him engages the grace of our redemption in Christ to clear us of our wrongdoing. We should make confession of sin a regular part of our personal prayer. Catholics should make frequent use of the Sacrament of Reconciliation. When our sin affects others, we may need to repair our relationship with

them by admitting our bad behavior and asking forgiveness. If we have damaged someone's reputation or property, we must make every effort to restore it.

We should have sorrow for our sin, which means grieving over having offended God. However, God does not want us to heap excessive blame on ourselves. We should not condemn ourselves, an attitude which is self-oriented. Self-condemnation is actually not sorrow but another common emotional problem called feeling bad about yourself.

Mary's Story

These three steps deal with sin simply and directly. They clear us of guilt because they eliminate its cause. Repentance is dynamic. We turn from sin and in the momentum of that dramatic, sweeping curve, we turn to the Lord. The Lord himself is not idle. He penetrates our guilt, using it to invite us to come back to him. He acknowledges our repentance and forgives us.

At first, we may not feel very forgiven. Guilt is strong medicine and sometimes it leaves an unpleasant aftertaste. We may feel guilty after the substance of guilt has been dissolved by repentance. If we continue to have guilt feelings over wrongdoing which the Lord has forgiven, we must immerse ourselves in his mercy.

Mary's story is both instructive and encouraging. Mary was an aged patient, confined to a nursing home by Parkinson's disease. She was profoundly unhappy, something that her constant state of withdrawal announced to all. On one wintery Sunday during a blizzard, Lillian, a social worker who was acquainted with Mary, felt drawn to visit the home and speak to Mary. She found the old lady in her room, weeping.

"Mary, do you want to tell me why you are crying?" asked Lillian. Mary pulled Lillian closer, motioned her to the chair opposite her, and said, "Why did you come here today?"

"Mary, I don't know. All I know is that I am here. Why don't you tell me why you are crying?"

"Well," Mary said, "I've been thinking about death, and I'm terribly afraid. Do you really believe God forgives our sins?"

"Yes, Mary," replied the social worker, "I not only believe, I know God forgives us. Is there some terrible sin you have committed that you think God cannot forgive?"

"Yes," answered Mary, and she began to cry again.

Slowly, punctuating her sentences with sobs, Mary told Lillian her painful secret. She had lived for nearly fifty years with a man she had never married. Guilt gnawed at her constantly. Having the respect of family and friends made her feel hypocritical and intensified her self-condemnation.

"About five years before my husband died, he became ill with cancer," said Mary. "I prayed and prayed for a miracle. Then one day he asked to see a priest, saying he wanted to become a Catholic. A short time before he died he was baptized, confessed his sins, received the eucharist, and we were married."

"Have you carried this burden alone all these years, Mary?" Lillian asked.

"Yes."

"What about confession? I'm sure you have talked to a priest about this."

"I asked for forgiveness, and the priest told me God had forgiven me. But I have never been able to stop feeling uncertain about it all. Would God really forgive me?"

Lillian assured Mary that she was forgiven. Then she took

Mary's hands in hers, with tears falling softly upon them, and asked the Lord to give Mary the peace of mind that had eluded her for so many years.

A glimmer of hope shone in Mary's eyes. "If I die tomorrow, will Jesus be standing by my bed to take me by the hand?" she asked.

"Yes, Mary, I know he will."

At eight o'clock that very night Mary died peacefully of a stroke. God had healed guilt's ugly wound.

Opening ourselves to God's mercy dissipates the residue of our guilt. Mother Angelica, the contemplative nun who runs a Christian cable television network, tells this story. Once, as she was standing near the sea's edge, a wave doused her. As she looked at a droplet on her finger, she thought she heard the Lord say, "Angelica, do you see this drop?"

"Yes, Lord."

"It represents all of your sins." Then the Lord directed her eyes to the sea. "Angelica, do you see this vast ocean?"

"Yes, I see it Lord," she said.

"It represents my mercy towards you. If you were to fling that drop into the ocean, do you think you could ever find it again?"

"Not a chance," said Angelica.

"The same is true about your droplet of sins and the ocean of my mercy," said the Lord. "You can keep the drop and let it make you miserable, or you can lose it forever in my mercy. What shall it be?"

So Angelica flung both drops into both seas.

What shall it be for us? Shall we hang on to our sins and let guilt devour us? Or shall we turn away from sin in order to turn fully to the Lord?

FOUR

Disappointment

DISAPPOINTMENT HAS BEEN A MAJOR ELEMENT in the human condition for a long time. Imagine this conversation between Adam and Eve, just after being dismissed from Paradise:

> ADAM: Eve, I'm very disappointed in you. I counted on you to help me, and you really let me down.
> EVE: You're disappointed?! What about me? What do I have to look forward to now? Nothing but drudgery and pain!

The same old things discourage us that disappointed our ancestors. Here's a check list to help you sort out some of the sources of our disappointment:

Failure. Recently, a television movie told the story of a high school senior who committed suicide because he felt he did not measure up in competence and confidence to the rest of his family. In addition, the boy felt he was a failure because he could not have everything he wanted. He had his heart set on romance with the prettiest, most sophisticated girl in school, and she regarded him as one of many "nice boys" who were "just friends."

We experience failure in many ways, but two are pre-eminent. We get discouraged when we fail to *acquire* something we have been determined to have. We look forward to possessing something—a house, a car—or to enjoying a certain pleasure or a relationship with someone. When it doesn't come, disappointment arrives in its place.

We also feel disappointed when we fail to *achieve* a goal that we set or that someone sets for us. We may not get the grades in school, reach the quotas at work, or attain the standards of excellent housekeeping set by our mothers.

Failure comes in the large economy size, too. The plumber or executive who is fired after twenty years of service may lose his sense of achievement and self-confidence overnight. What do divorced people see but failure in the train wreck that is left of the family life which they had invested so heavily in?

Loss. Closely related to this is disappointment caused by the loss of something that meant a lot to us. Recently a thief entered our home and took my wife's purse. Mary Lou lost several photographs of our children that could mean nothing to the culprit but were dear to her. She got over her anger at the loss of money and at the inconvenience easily, but she is still disappointed over the loss of the photos.

The dearer the lost object is to us, the deeper the discouragement we feel. What is more painful than the loss of a child? We all know people whose disappointment over the death of a son or daughter has bent their lives in whole new directions. The direction may be good because sometimes tragedies draw families together and result in strengthened relationships and greater faith. The direction, however, is too often bad. Disappointment over a child's death, or of someone close to us, can readily grow into bigger problems like self-pity and despair.

Change. Unanticipated change is another source of disappointment. After all the children grow up and move out, parents may experience "the empty nest syndrome" and get discouraged. Elderly people are especially vulnerable to changes either big or small. My father-in-law retired early. In one day he went from an active, productive life to a life of sedentary discouragement. I think deep-seated disappointment was a factor in his death.

Double-cross. When something does not go the way we expect, we feel disappointed. Mary Catherine, our three-year-old, always counts on riding along in the car with Mary Lou or me. When we go somewhere and leave her behind, she feels double-crossed. She expresses her disappointment vividly with dramatic pouts.

Adults may react the same way on a grander scale. When I took my master's exam, the unexpected happened. I flunked it. Since I had reduced my study time in order to do Christian service, I felt double-crossed. I blamed God for the failure. Like Mary Catherine I put on a dramatic pout—for two years.

Our disappointment often focuses on a person who falls short of our expectations. My father was a good baseball player and had also played on a championship sandlot soccer team. Imagine the disappointment I was to him when one day at age eleven I dropped out of little league because I could neither catch nor hit. And if Vince McColligan had not caught the high fly ball that was about to land square on my forehead that day, you might not have the benefit of this book. Our disappointment is worse when we discover that a favorite uncle is an alcoholic or when a lifelong friend turns against us.

There are other sources of disappointment not described here, among them illness, injury, and rejection. By this point, you get the picture and may be identifying some of the things that have caused you the most discouragement.

The Social Disease of the '80s

In a *U.S. News & World Report* interview, psychologist David Brandt predicted that "disappointment may be the social disease of the '80s." He based his observation on data which demonstrates that expectations may never have been higher and broader than they are in America. I think Brandt is correct.

The media is the factor that makes the difference. The media builds us up for the big letdowns. Anyone who watches even a little television exposes himself regularly to programming and commercials that tell him he can have anything he wants in life. The beer commercial says it all with the line, "Who says you can't have it all without losing your soul?" With all the wreckage about, one would think that the producers and advertising agencies would realize that the idea of progress—the myth that things always get better and better—crashed on the rocks of reality shortly after that ill-fated notion first crossed someone's mind.

We live in a time of exaggerated expectations. And the bigger the expectations, the bigger the disappointments.

Good Advice

How can we avoid disappointment or at least reduce it when we can't escape from it? There is plenty of good advice available. If we're smart, we'll take it. David Brandt, for example, told readers of *U.S. News* to "recognize that every wish is not possible" and to keep expectations "flexible." Desires can be good, but they must be kept in line with reality, much as I must not write checks in excess of what is really in my bank account.

The Ghezzi children (four boys, three girls) have been Pittsburgh Steelers fans ever since they could crawl. Their mother, the athlete, infected them with sports fever. Seven of us spent Thanksgiving 1983 in the Pontiac Silverdome, fully expecting the Steelers to make mincemeat of the Detroit Lions, our second favorite football team. It was an unforgettable game. We would have been better off with more "flexible" expectations, as the Lions gobbled up the Steelers and spit out the bones. My eldest son was so disappointed that for days he refused the evidence of reality, arguing that it must not have been the Steelers on the field after all.

Dr. Brandt also advises us to "pursue goals that are consistent with our abilities. It makes no sense expecting to be a translator of French novels if we're not very good at foreign languages." I am reminded of a response one of my professors once made to an undergraduate who wanted to know what it would take for him to earn an "A" in his western civilization class. It was the week before final exams and the young man had earned straight "Ds" and "Fs." After offering to write extra papers, to read additional books and so on, the persistent fellow hit the professor with the ultimate question: "What if I ace the final exam?"

"What if I win the Nobel Prize for Literature?" asked the exasperated professor.

Not all the advice we get from counselors is as sound as Dr. Brandt's. When we find good suggestions, we should adopt them. We should leave bad advice lying where we found it. Also, we should not expect more of this kind of help than it offers. There is an ever-expanding body of techniques designed to aid us in our quest for emotional health. Such techniques mostly deal with symptoms, like aspirin for headaches, but they are not cures. Let's not expect more of them than they can claim, and we will not be doubly disappointed.

A lady once wrote me an angry letter, saying that my trivial examples showed I didn't really understand discouragement. Her anger expressed a profound unhappiness that came from a sense of utter failure. She and her husband had built their marriage on solid Christian principles. More than anything, they had wanted their children to turn out right, so they studied about child-rearing, learned from experienced parents, and involved themselves in a Christian family movement. They worked hard at providing their children a Christian home. They believed they were doing what God wanted, and they probably were.

Twenty years later every child was a disappointment. Some were on drugs; some had illegitimate children; one divorced; and another was a twice-convicted felon, serving a jail term. Many parents are in pain, but this family seems to have had an extra dose of trouble. The lady was understandably discouraged. How can we face such depressing events? Is there any way out of holes so deep as this one seems to be? Where is God when we need him? Why does he let things like this happen to people who love him?

Deep discouragement is hard to shake off because it makes us feel like giving up, running away, or even taking our own life. In the face of severe disappointment, steps like lowering expectations or keeping aspirations in line appear to be too minor to be of help. Depressed people don't think God is very interested in them, so they find it very difficult to approach him about their problems. But if we turn to him even a little, we will begin to see a way out.

FIVE

Turning to God in Surrender

AS GOOD AS THE SECULAR ADVICE on handling disappointment is, it is merely three-dimensional. It can only show us how to rearrange circumstances so we are less uncomfortable. It can only teach us how to lower our standards, so that people measure up better and we can be less disappointed by them. These are good devices and we should use them.

Christians, however, have additional means for handling disappointment. The Christian approaches are multi-dimensional. They were given to us by Christ, and they are inspired by the Holy Spirit. They can get beneath the surface to the cause of the discouragement.

Humility. Humility is an attitude which acts as a preventive against disappointment. Sometimes we confuse humility with feeling-bad-about-ourselves, or worse, with self-pity. These two are emotional problems that masquerade as humility but really have very little to do with the virtue.

Humility has two defining elements—sober self-judgment and heartfelt service. Scripture teaches that we must have an accurate assessment of ourselves so that we neither belittle ourselves and do less than God wants of us, nor think more highly of ourselves than we ought, thus ending up a disappointment to everyone.

Mother Angelica says repeatedly that she is not afraid to fail, but she is afraid to die and face a God who may have to say, "Angelica, let me show you what you could have done." That's humility. That's a humble person who thinks of herself with sober judgment according to the measure of faith God gave her (Rom 12:3).

Humility also involves dedicated service of others. A humble person devotes himself to caring for others, as Jesus did. He always thinks of himself as a servant. He looks for what those around him need and then does it (Phil 2:4). A humble person has not got much time to think about himself, so he dramatically reduces the possibility of disappointment. He's too busy loving others to be bothered with it.

Practically speaking, when we are feeling discouraged, we should ask God's help and look for someone we can help. Prayer puts us in touch with God's Spirit, bringing spiritual help to us. Service engages the biblical principle which can dissolve our disappointment in the joy of giving to others.

Forgiveness. I saw a bumper sticker recently that declared, "I don't get mad, I get even." There is a school of secular advice that could march proudly beneath that banner. Those who preach the doctrines of "looking out for number one" and asserting ourselves against others part company with Christians at the fork in the road marked "Forgiveness."

More often than not, our disappointment is a by-product

of our relationships with others. We are less than we think our dad wanted us to be or one of our own children has stopped speaking to us. We overhear a friend speaking against us. One spouse discovers the other's infidelity. We may get angry when such things happen, and it may be right to do so. We may become discouraged as well. But as Christians we must not get even.

The plain teaching of Scripture is that Christians must forgive those who offend them. Peter once asked Jesus, "How often shall my brother sin against me, and I forgive him? As many as seven times?" We all know Jesus' answer, which conveys the heart of the message: always. "I do not say to you seven times, but seventy times seven" (Mt 18:22). How many of us, hardhearted as we are, have been tempted to count up to 491?

We all know the teaching, but somehow we have forgotten how to do it. In my experience, too many Christians do not know how to say "I'm sorry" when they have wronged somebody. It is even more rare to find a Christian who says "I forgive you" to a person who is asking forgiveness of them.

Let's start asking and giving forgiveness right in our own families and among our closest circle of friends. We can teach each other that when we offend someone we must say to the injured party "please forgive me" for whatever we did wrong. We should expect each other to say "you're forgiven" when someone asks us to be forgiven some offense. These acts of seeking and granting forgiveness repair offenses and restore relationships. Hurt feelings can then begin to mend because we've cleared away the junk.

Christians who ask and grant forgiveness find other people a lot less disappointing than those who do not.

The Antidote

There are secular techniques and Christian ways of dealing with disappointment. There is an antidote for it. God revealed it to us. Like other pieces of revelation, however, something had to happen to drive it home to me.

I discovered it about thirteen years ago during one of the worst months in Ghezzi family history. To begin with, I was overextended, working two jobs and serving in two charismatic renewal groups in two towns, thirty-five miles apart. My wife had contracted pleurisy and was confined to bed. We had four children then, and one by one they were attacked by a rip-roaring virus. I was the only healthy person around, so I was trying to care for the whole mess.

One would think that if God was trying to say something to me, he had let enough happen to catch my attention. But no, what really got to me was that, on top of everything else, the cat infested the entire house with fleas! The whole state of affairs discouraged me deeply. I was angry with everyone and everything, and especially furious with God for allowing this string of misfortunes to overtake me.

A friend had given me an audiocassette of a talk by Bob Mumford, my favorite Pentecostal teacher, saying that I might find his message helpful. So, one evening in the midst of all this, having forced myself not to commit mayhem on the cat, I stood in the kitchen drying dishes and folding clothes while I listened to the tape.

Mumford was speaking about Christians who were profoundly unhappy in their circumstances. Since I was profoundly unhappy in mine, I perked up and listened even more carefully. He was telling about an experience he had once in a southern town. One day as he was walking downtown, he stopped to observe a scene across the street.

An old man was patiently stroking a cat. Now that caught my attention, since I knew of a cat I'd like to stroke.

I am told that most cats like to be stroked. It calms them and causes them to purr. This cat, however, was definitely not purring. It was hissing, complaining loudly and pawing the pavement. As Mumford drew closer, he immediately saw why. The old man was stroking the cat from back to front, rubbing it the wrong way. He was saying something softly to the cat. Mumford bent over to listen. The man was whispering over and over: "Turn around, cat!"

Mumford then observed that the man was actually stroking the cat the right way, but the cat was standing in the wrong position in relation to the man.

At first, I did not like the conclusion Bob Mumford was drawing. For one thing, at that moment I did not like being compared to a cat, any cat. Mumford said that when bad things happen to a Christian and he complains, and hisses, and kicks his feet up in anger, it may be that he is not standing in the right relation to God. After all, he said, like the old man in the story, God knows how to care for us. If he strokes us, he is doing it the right way. If the strokes irritate instead of soothe us, maybe we need to turn around, like the cat in the anecdote. That may be the very reason God decided to stroke us.

In the midst of all the pressures, illnesses, chores, and fleas, I heard the Lord speaking to me. "Bert Ghezzi," he seemed to say, "are you willing to accept the circumstances of your life on my terms?" If yes, I knew I could grow closer to him. If no, I knew I would remain in my disappointment and may be in for more. So I repented for my bitter attitude toward God, and I began to approach the series of difficulties more peacefully.

When the circumstances of life seem to go bad all at

once—when we are profoundly disappointed—we should listen to the word of God and repent. Repentance at root means a turning around. A turning away from rebellion and a turning to God. Acknowledging God's sovereignty is the Christian antidote for the deepest discouragement.

Surrender to God

Once I was complaining to a friend about some circumstances in my life. My car was always breaking down, the house I was living in did not have enough play area for my children, finances were tight, one of my children wasn't doing what I expected of them, and so on. My friend heard me out and then said, "You really don't have anything that you should be complaining about, Bert. You offered your life to the Lord and have been trying to serve him. Sometimes Jesus takes what we offer him and doesn't say 'thanks.'"

My mistake is a common one. You may have made it, too. I tell the Lord that I am surrendering my life to him. I trust that since God listens and wants my life, he accepts the offer. However, at one moment I put him in charge of me, and in the next I am trying to get things to work out the way I want them. That's why circumstances vex me. My preferences conflict with the Lord's.

There is a law of physics which says that two objects cannot occupy the same space at the same time. There is a similar spiritual law that says God and I cannot be in charge of my life at the same time. I cannot have it both ways, surrendering to the Lord and having things my way, just as you and I cannot stand on the same spot at the same time.

Surrendering to the Lord means putting him first and eliminating all competition for first place, including ourselves. The apostle Paul did it in exemplary fashion, but it was not easy for him either. He was, as he said to the Philippians, "circumcised on the eighth day, of the people of Israel, of the tribe of Benjamin, a Hebrew born of Hebrews; as to the law a Pharisee, as to zeal a persecutor of the church, as to righteousness under the law blameless." Paul had many advantages—he had a lot going for him. But when he became the Lord's servant, he cleared the way for the Lord to govern his life. "But whatever gain I had," he wrote, "I counted as loss for the sake of Christ" (Phil 3:5-7).

Paul's emphasis and his choice of words in the subsequent verses suggest that he had to discipline his thoughts to prevent himself from seizing control from the Lord. He says, "Indeed I *count* everything as loss because of the surpassing worth of knowing Christ Jesus my Lord. For his sake I have suffered the loss of all things, and count them as *refuse*, in order that I may gain Christ and be found in him" (Phil 3:8-9). I would do well to imitate Paul more closely. You would, too. For example, when my preferences push themselves forward, inciting me to compete with the Lord, I ought to remind myself that with Paul I have lost everything in order to gain Christ. Paul uses the word "count," suggesting keeping strict accounts in a ledger, and the word here translated "refuse" can be rendered accurately as "dung." We ought to hold ourselves to the same accounting, saying in our mind, this thing I yearn for is dung compared to the inestimable value of knowing Christ Jesus.

The Practicality of Thanksgiving

In one of his letters Paul gives a series of commands which at first glance seem absurd. "Rejoice always, pray constantly, give thanks in all circumstances" (1 Thes 5:16-18). I know people who have tried to pray constantly, for example, and kept it up for about a day and a half, except when they slept. Applying the text literally is simply impossible. Upon reflection, however, we can appreciate the practicality of the commands. They point to our relationship with the Lord, and they bring us into touch with the power of the Holy Spirit. They are practical because they are impossible to obey without surrendering ourselves more fully to God.

The circumstances of daily life are a training ground in letting God have his way. They are opportunities for Christians to stop expecting everything to go according to their own plans. Giving thanks is the means of our surrender on each occasion.

Ever since I can remember, each summer from June through August, from 4 PM until 9 PM most nights, I am occupied as a chauffeur for my children. I really ought to have a cap with a glossy black brim. You may be able to tell that I don't like the job very much. Recently, I dropped off one son at work and was driving down the freeway to pick up another. It was very hot and humid and I was very tired and cross. All of a sudden there was a loud explosion as my left rear tire burst and a bang! bang! bang! as I swerved onto the shoulder. There I was in my best suit, having to change a tire with traffic racing at my back.

That wasn't all. I had recently bought this second hand station wagon, a junker, to save money, right? A tune-up and spare tire had just cost me $100. The banging noise, I discovered as gasoline began to trickle onto the asphalt, had been my gas tank bouncing on the road. Now I would have to purchase new tires *and* a gas tank. I barely resisted the temptation to say sarcastically, "Thanks, Lord, I needed this!"

Instead, I began to thank the Lord for allowing this frustrating circumstance. As I prayed, I recalled that just two days earlier I had driven my four sons sixty miles at high speeds to a Detroit Tiger baseball game. My wife had used the car all day transporting the younger children around the city. A blowout in either of these situations could have been life-threatening. So I found myself praying, rejoicing in God's protection, and thanking him for my inconvenience. The net effect was that I was a little more surrendered to God.

Thanksgiving is also a practical way to yield to God's will in more serious situations. That's why he trains us on the lesser matters. For example, in *Sometimes Mountains Move,* C. Everett and Elizabeth Koop write about the tragic death of their twenty-year-old son David, who fell to his death while rock climbing in the White Mountains of New Hampshire. The testimony was written only a few months after David's death. The Koop family impressed me with their acceptance of this tragedy; they were surrendered to God's sovereignty. The most intriguing quality of their response was their thankfulness. They write about how thankful they were for David, for his contributions to their life, and how they appreciated all the ways the Lord prepared David for death and the family for losing him. There is a connection between their gracious acceptance of God's will and their thankfulness.

Thankfulness in all circumstances bends our will to God's. It is the instrument of our surrender.

SIX

Lust and Other Disorderly Desires

MOST GRADUATION ADDRESSES are not memorable, but I will never forget Arzie Harris's speech at my son Paul's high school commencement. The principal said he was pleased to introduce Arzie, the senior class president, who would make a few remarks. I have already forgotten these observations, which were mostly superficialities about the year that had passed. But, what did stick in my mind was Arzie's closing exhortation: "Be greedy," he urged. "Go after whatever you want because there's nobody out there looking out for you except yourself."

Not very logical, Arzie, I muttered. If his classmates, some of whom I knew well, were to pursue their heart's desires without restraint, they would land in jail. But I gave Arzie a high mark for accuracy. He had distilled the essence of our culture's message, and in a single sentence he had proposed it as a toast to his classmates' future.

The message is flawed, but I don't fault Arzie, who was only a messenger, or even the culture for it. Where do slogans like "go for it—you deserve it," "have it your way," and "look out for number one" originate? Why do songwriters repeatedly equate love and desire in verses like, "I want you, baby, I can't live without you?" How do ad agencies conclude that appeals to sexual desire will sell anything from breath mints to garage door openers? Why do they think we would respond to extravagance celebrated under the rubric, "MasterCard, I love you?"

The spokesmen of our culture get their ideas by consulting us. They are not physicians, prescribing bitter medicine which they force us to take for our own good. They are more like fortune-tellers, who try to tell us exactly what they discern we want to hear. Their slogans reflect the desires they find in our hearts. No wonder we respond with enthusiasm to the images they set before us.

The anticipation of pleasure is the aspect of desire that fascinates us, and that is the part that advertisers appeal to. Lust, greed, and envy offer us prizes which we enjoy savoring before we get them. Recently, for example, I saw an advertisement in a sports magazine for a certain brand of gin which promised that drinking it would be rewarded by intimacy with a pretty girl. The ad deliberately appealed to the anticipation of sexual fulfillment, which is the coiled spring that makes lust dynamic.

Lust and other compulsive desires are masters of the double cross. They offer pleasures which we long for, but when we get the desired objects, they rarely match our expectations. For example, a man addicted to pornography may look to magazines and films for the ultimate in sexual delight, only to subject himself to degradations of sexual love which leave him feeling cheated and ashamed. Or parents who have an excessive desire to manipulate their children may find that they have destroyed the very relationship they had wanted to dominate.

Unruly desires are not easily satisfied. They draw us,

incite us, drive us. That's why when the object of our longing disappoints us, desire goes right back to work, perhaps with even greater intensity, promoting our interest in something else that promises to delight us. For example, people who covet fancy sports cars may discover that the vehicles do not make them as content as they expected, and they may then hanker after sailboats, jacuzzis, and other extravagances. Note that you don't have to be wealthy for this principle to work. Recently, I replaced my old instamatic with an automatic 35 millimeter camera. I like the new camera very much, but instead of being content, I find myself wanting a more sophisticated camera which is three times as expensive. Disorderly desires offer you everything you ever wanted, and give you less.

Desires and the Christian Life

Unruly desires are more troublesome for us when we take Christianity seriously. We notice the stirrings of greed or lust more because they bend us in directions that offend God. However, we must not conclude that all desire tends to evil and, therefore, must be eliminated from our lives, a mistake that some good Christians made in the past.

God made desires good, and they are an integral part of our human nature. An informal survey of ordinary desires would include many which move us in naturally good directions. Newlyweds want to make love and get their new life together off to a good start. Mothers and fathers want to protect and care for their children. Girls and boys desire to achieve well in school and long to be able to make their own decisions. Even sexual desire, which we fear always leads to trouble, is radically good. Without it we would not bother to propagate the race.

Our survey would also list desires that specifically support good Christian living. We may discover that we have a strong desire to spend time praying; to study scripture so that we can know the Lord better; to spend time helping the poor; to tell people whom we love about Jesus; or to work for prison reform or for some other form of social justice. Like automobiles which perform better when their machinery is well lubricated, we are more effective as Christians when our desires work with us rather than against us.

Disorderly Desires

An inventory of ordinary desires will disclose some which incline us to bad thoughts and bad behavior. These are disorderly desires, and the following list describes some of the more prominent ones.

Lust is excessive sexual desire or sexual desire which is focused on a person or deed that God's law forbids. The term covers everything from impure thoughts to rape.

Greed is an excessive desire to have or to acquire things. It includes a range of thoughts and deeds, from cupidity to robbery.

Power involves wanting to control another's life. "Lust for power" is a common name for this desire. This unruly passion inclines us to prying, meddling, manipulation, and tyrannical behavior.

Hatred is a strong feeling of dislike for someone, and may result in ill will, conflict, injury, and even murder.

Envy and its close companions, covetousness and jealousy, involves an ardent longing for the qualities, advantages, achievements, or possessions that belong to another. It springs from comparing ourselves to others and concluding that we don't measure up to them. Covetousness specifies envy for another's possessions. Jealousy is envy at work in relationships. We resent a person who rivals or who seems to threaten our place in the affections of someone who means a lot to us. Envy and its associates may be shot through with enmity.

All of us have feelings and thoughts that fall into these categories, but that alone does not mean we have a problem with disorderly desires. Lust, for example, may regularly strike up conversations with us. But sexual desires, even if they're done in Panavision and Dolby Stereo, are not harmful if they are just passing by. When they begin to hang around, we may have reason to be concerned.

Let's take another example. Envy may prompt occasional feelings that we are more deserving than someone else. We may wish that we had been promoted to manager instead of our colleague; or that we had married our neighbor's husband; or that we had been valedictorian of our class. These are merely temptations to envy, which we can dismiss as we would any other unworthy but dangerous thought.

But suppose we begin to play with the thoughts. We imagine what it would be like if we were in the position of the person we envied: we would be a more effective manager, or a more loving wife, or a more worthy valedictorian. We remember a comment the person once made. It had seemed innocent at the time, but now, colored by our envious feelings, it seems to have been a deliberate putdown. Resentment engages us, and we may begin to speak or act with a coldness which communicates our feelings to the person we envy. By now envy has assumed its status as a disorderly desire.

It takes work for a desire to become unruly. The desire must work on us and we must work at it. Fleeting thoughts must harden into dominant passions. So, our desires become disorderly when they fascinate us and impel us to evil deeds.

When Are Disorderly Desires Sinful?

Disorderly desires are not automatically sinful, but they set us on an inclined plane which slides into sin. If feelings of lust, greed, or envy incite us to action, some sin is almost certainly involved.

Unruly passions may become sinful thoughts even before we express them in evil deeds. It's hard to tell when we have crossed the line between evil tendency and sin in our thoughts, because the boundary is indistinct. There are, however, some clues. Jesus said, for example, that "everyone who looks at a woman lustfully has already committed adultery with her in his heart" (Mt 5:28). To emphasize the seriousness of the matter, he also said, "If your right eye causes you to sin, pluck it out and throw it away; it is better that you lose one of your members than that your whole body be thrown into hell" (verse 29).

Since Christians, including biblical literalists, have rarely blinded themselves to resist lust, we can conclude that this passage has commonly been interpreted to mean that sometimes sexual thoughts stop short of sin. When do they become sinful? Suppose a person's mind is dominated by sexual fantasies; he decides to enhance them by looking at pornography; he meditates on the sexual images he has received; he begins to wish for sexual relations with someone; he begins to frequent places where he might meet someone, and so on. At what point did he cross the boundary line? Jesus says we sin when we imagine performing outlawed sexual deeds or decide we would do them if we had the opportunity.

When we take pleasure in our disorderly desires, we should suspect that we are stepping dangerously close to the line between bad tendency and sin. When we take steps to enhance them, we are close to crossing the boundary. When we ardently wish for a chance to satisfy the desire or formulate a plan of action, we have crossed it.

Discipline and Self-Denial

There are many ways to restrain disorderly desires. When we find one that works, we should use it. A young man once complained to a friend that summer was difficult for him because scantily dressed females triggered his sexual fantasies. "What do you think God made eyelids for?" she replied, scaling down Jesus' teaching on plucking out the eye. We may be able to reduce the power of lustful desires by limiting our exposure to materials that stimulate us sexually. If we know that certain people, places, publications, or films agitate our unruly passions, we should decide to avoid them.

Since disorderly desires originate as feelings or thoughts, mental discipline, if applied early enough, can check their development. For example, when thoughts of jealousy pass through our minds, we should see that they move right on out. We're in charge of what goes on in our minds; we should keep them swept clean of all dangerous thoughts.

Various forms of self-denial can strengthen our will for battle against disorderly desires. Fasting is an appropriate discipline for hardening our resistance to lust, just as living simply and giving generously to people in need can help us overcome greed.

Discipline and self-denial can subdue the intensity of disorderly desires. We ought to welcome whatever they can do, without expecting them to make more than a modest contribution. Radical healing of unruly desires requires us to strike at their source, at our self-indulgence.

Self-Indulgence

Arzie Harris's exhortation contained a clue to the root problem of disorderly desires. You recall his dictum, which I think ought to be ordained as Arzie Harris's Law of Beneficial Greed: "Be greedy and go after whatever you want, because there is nobody out there looking out for you except yourself." We should not quibble with the apparent absence of God from Arzie's universe, since here Arzie, who probably believes in God, was so focused on the self that he could not see anything else, even God. Take care of your *self*. Gratify your *self*. 'Tis self-indulgence, not love, that makes Arzie Harris's world go 'round. And perhaps ours, too.

Disorderly desires issue from hearts dominated by self-indulgence. The apostle Paul says that, "When self-indulgence is at work the results are obvious: fornication, gross indecency and sexual irresponsibility; idolatry and sorcery; feuds and wrangling, jealousy, bad temper and quarrels; disagreements, factions, envy; drunkenness, orgies and similar things. I warn you now, as I warned you before: those who behave like this will not inherit the kingdom of God" (Gal 5:19-21; JB).

Paul says that overcoming these unruly desires will take violence, for they will continue to reign unless we crucify our self-indulgence. We must turn from loving our *self* to loving God.

SEVEN

Turning to God's Love

THE PASTOR MENTIONED in chapter one was addicted to pornography. How did he get free? He says that the writings of Francois Mauriac, the Nobel prize-winning novelist, helped him break his habit and turn back to God. One of these books was *The Knot of Vipers*, a novel about lust, avarice, hatred, and revenge. Mauriac tells how these passions obscured a man's seeing the radiance of God and blocked his receiving God's mercy until the very end of his life. Here is a lesson about deliverance from the grasp of disorderly desires.

Mauriac tells the story of Louis, who is not a Christian, and his relationships with Isa, his wife, and their extended family, who profess to be devout Roman Catholics. Louis is afflicted with heart disease which has confined him to his room and which is about to claim his life. Isa and the family hate the old man and are waiting somewhat impatiently for his long-awaited death, which would release the fortune he has amassed and horded.

The novel takes the form of a long letter which Louis intends Isa to read upon his death. He surveys his miserable life, cataloging his grievances against his avaricious family. He tells how Isa's pride and hatefulness wore him down and fueled the furnace of his own problems. He had found comfort in the arms of other women. Greed had propelled his career as an attorney, another escape from Isa.

For years Louis had plotted revenge. He had formulated an intricate scheme to put his fortune beyond his family's reach. Their horror at the discovery of his vengeance would be his final amusement. But somehow, Louis says, he has gotten beyond his hatred and has decided to forego the trick. As death draws closer, he merely wants to let Isa know something of the man she has hated for forty years.

Louis understands Christianity better than Isa, and he has hated her religious formalism as a caricature. He longed to know God personally. At one point he says he is dying of hatred and cries out, "Oh God, if only You existed."[2] As death approaches, he finds himself relaxing his lifelong resistance to Christianity.

God had pursued Louis throughout his life, and in the end Louis wishes he had known God. The old man understands his situation clearly. Avarice and hatred are the real diseases of his heart. They have held him captive, tortured him, and soon will deliver their final, fatal sting. Only a God he claims not to believe in can intervene to deliver him. "I know my heart," he confesses, "it is a knot of vipers. They have almost squeezed the life out of it. They have beslavered it with their poison, but underneath their squirming, it still beats. Impossible now to loosen the knot. I can fight free only by cutting it with a knife, by slashing it with a sword: *I am come to bring not peace but a sword.*"[3]

Just before his death, Louis begins occasionally to experience God's presence. "Stripped of everything," he says once, "isolated, and with a terrible death hanging over my head, I remained calm.... It was as though I were not a sick old man, as though I still had a lifetime before me, as though the peace of which I was possessed was Somebody."[4] At the last moment, we are aware that the Lord has intervened with mercy and violence, penetrating the tiny fissure in Louis's heart, which the old man seems to have opened himself. Louis dies while writing these words in his letter: "Something is stifling me, something is making my heart feel as though it would burst—it is the Love whose name at last I know, whose ardor...."[5]

The Cure for Heart Disease

The Knot of Vipers expands our understanding of God's love and of human passions. Let's enumerate some of the truths which Mauriac depicts in Louis's demise:

1. Unruly passions can ruin our lives.
2. They can be a wall that blocks our view of God and prevents us from knowing his mercy. Once Louis reminds Isa of all the "greedy desires which had stood between her and the Eternal Being."
3. In their advanced stages, lust and greed poison and constrict our hearts so that God must resort to violence, which is symbolized by the sword that Jesus came to bring.
4. If the afflicted person opens his heart ever so slightly, God's love breaks in with deliverance.

When avarice, lust, and other disorderly desires have stunned us into submission, our real problem is spiritual heart disease. Jesus said: "From within, out of the heart of man, come evil thoughts, fornication, theft, murder, adultery, coveting, wickedness, deceit, licentiousness, envy, slander, pride, foolishness. All these evil things come from within, and they defile a man" (Mk 7:21-23). Note the similarity between this passage and the Galatians 5 passage cited when we pinpointed self-indulgence as the root problem behind unruly desires. Our spiritual heart disease is self-indulgence. Envy, impurity, greed, and other hideous desires stream from hearts dedicated to self, and they befoul us as they bear fruit in evil behavior.

Jesus teaches that the heart is paramount in orienting our lives either for evil or for good. To grasp this, we may have to broaden our understanding of the word heart. Contemporary popular culture tends to identify our heart with our feelings. In popular songs, for example, a pretty girl is always said to steal a boy's *heart* away. Almost without fail, this means he feels so attracted to her that there is no room in his attention for anything else. When Jesus talks about our heart—as in the text "you shall love the Lord your God with all your heart" (Mt 22:37)—he is not referring to feelings like this but to something much deeper. The book of Proverbs tells us to "keep your heart with all vigilance; for from it flow the springs of life" (4:23). Another translation says the heart contains "the sources of life." The heart is the deep center, from which spring motivation, intention, and decision. It directs the feelings, will, and reason, which act as its external agents.

When the Lord pursues us, as he did Louis in the novel, he comes after our heart. He wants the heart because he wants everything, and everything comes with the heart. When he finds our heart encircled by a knot of unruly passions and dominated by a tyrannical self-indulgence, he is determined to cut us free, if we show the least openness to him. That's the meaning of the Scripture passages about circumcision of the heart, which may sound strange to us. "And the Lord your God will circumcise your heart and the heart of your offspring, so that you will love the Lord your God with all your heart and with all your soul, that you may live" (Dt 30:6). "Real circumcision," said Paul, "is a matter of the heart, spiritual and not literal" (Rom 2:29).

Physical circumcision is a painful operation, and spiritual circumcision hurts no less. Disorderly desires afflict the soul with waves of emotional and spiritual pain. On top of that, there is the pain of the spiritual circumcision, the additional pain God brings as he cuts us free—the pain of conviction, cleansing, and change.

The Lord lays hold of hearts that are entangled by greed and lust so that he can reorient them to himself. Spiritual circumcision, according to Scripture, releases us to love God singleheartedly. God dethrones self from its place of dominance so that we can begin to love him from our heart.

Loving God from the Heart

What does it mean to love God from the heart? As a youth, I thought it meant strictly obeying his commandments. There is a strong element of truth in that idea. Jesus said, "If you keep my commandments, you will abide in my love, just as I have kept my Father's commandments and abide in his love" (Jn 15:10). The view is not incorrect, but it is incomplete, as I discovered later.

When I was twenty-three years old I made a retreat, called a cursillo, which means "short course" in Christianity. On that weekend, I made an adult commitment to follow Jesus, but I also learned many valuable truths, the most important being what it meant to love God from the heart. It was clear that the people who presented the cursillo loved God more deeply than I did. They loved him with warmth, with abandon, even wastefully. They had not stopped with mere obedience, but they loved God generously and affectionately. The test which verified this for me was the depth of their personal worship and their selfless service of other people.

Now I can see more easily how love-as-obeying-the-rules can deteriorate into religious formalism. Like Isa in Mauriac's story, Christians who equate love and obedience follow all the rules, but they may easily drift into a heartless Christianity, where there is not much love for anyone at all, including God.

On that cursillo weekend, I decided that I wanted to love God as these people did. So I imitated them. I prayed more, and I prayed more conversationally. I spoke to the Lord personally, telling him what was on my heart. Yes, I was aware that he already knew it, but speaking of my love for him made that love grow even more. I still pray this way twenty-two years later. I also found that singing certain choruses which celebrate the love of the Lord evoked heartfelt love from me. This kind of song still punctuates my personal prayer. Recently, for example, I have been using a very simple, moving song, which says over and over again:

> Lord, you are more precious than silver;
> Lord, you are more costly than gold;
> Lord, you are more beautiful than diamonds;
> Nothing I desire compares with you.

I am reminded of the old man who was observed praying in church. He would come early every morning and kneel for an hour or so, apparently doing nothing but keeping his eyes on the altar. A lady who was intrigued by him for several months finally stirred herself to ask him what he did when he prayed. The old man said, like someone very much in love, "I look at him and he looks at me." When I pray, I try to be like that man, so I can love the Lord even more.

Love of God and Disorderly Desires

Once we have turned to the Lord and begin to grow in loving him, wholesome desires, motives, and intentions will flow from our heart. Our disorderly desires will also begin to change. Some will be entirely defanged. Others will be easier to control. However, the Lord may allow us to struggle with some unruly passion, even after our surrender, as a reminder that his grace is enough for us.

Seventeen years ago, a man I will call Ted was deeply involved in the homosexual society of San Francisco. He worked as a ticket-taker at a pornographic cinema. He dabbled in transvestism and, in short, was pretty committed to the gay scene.

In 1970, he paid a polite visit to family members in a midwestern town. He arrived during a charismatic prayer meeting and cautiously tried to blend in along the fringes. God spoke to Ted's heart that night. He turned dramatically from his homosexuality and to a life of living for God. Ted never returned to San Francisco but stayed near his family and built a whole new life. He is now happily married, the father of three, and has worked in Christian service for fifteen years.

Homosexual desires are often compulsive and are among the most resistant to change, especially for people who have immersed themselves in the homosexual subculture. Ted's prospects were not good. However, the more Ted loved God, the more his homosexual desires were transformed. But they did not disappear. They de-escalated from the rank of unruly passions, which had dominated him, to difficult temptations, which he must still periodically fight. Why didn't the Lord change his desires completely? Shall we quibble with a God who saved a man who was fast sliding to his own doom and who now serves him well on the front lines, homosexual temptations and all? Let's not.

What about the pastor, mentioned at the beginning of the chapter, who was addicted to pornography? For a decade this passion drove him to sample all kinds of pornography, from magazines to striptease shows. The beginning of his deliverance came on his way to preach a retreat. He had wandered into a porn shop and viewed "live" nude girls in a twenty-five-cent booth. This time his revulsion and remorse numbed him. After the retreat, he sought help from his friend, only to find that his life had been ruined by sexual sin. When the pastor saw what lust had done to this excellent man, he glimpsed his own fate which awaited him only a few years down the road. The wreckage of this other pastor's life occasioned a turning point for him.

Circumstances then conspired to awaken him anew to God's love. Among these were Mauriac's works, including *A Knot of Vipers*, which put everything in the right perspective for him. Mauriac drew his attention to Jesus' teaching in the Sermon on the Mount: Blessed are the pure in heart, for they shall see God (Mt 5:8). He realized that he had so filled his heart with lustful images that there was scarcely any room left for love of God.

> The thought hit me like a bell rung in a dark, silent hall. So far, none of the scary, negative arguments against lust had succeeded in keeping me from it. Fear and guilt simply did not give me the resolve; they added self-hatred

to my problems. But here was a description of what I was missing by continuing to harbor lust: I was limiting my own intimacy with God. The love he offers is so transcendent and possessing that it requires our faculties to be purified and cleansed before we can possibly contain it.[6]

Turning back to God involved a painful but necessary step. The pastor wrote: "Repentance, says C.S. Lewis, 'is not something God demands of you before He will take you back and which He could let you off if He chose; it is simply a description of what going back is like.' Going back for me had to include a very long talk with my wife, who had suffered in silence and often in nescience for a decade. It was she I had wronged and sinned against, as well as God."[7] Late one summer's night he told his wife the whole story, and strengthened by God's grace, she was able to forgive him.

A year after he turned to God, the pastor says his unruly passion has lost its compulsive character. He is still tempted, but not driven. His lust, which had made God look distant and weak, is now dwarfed and diffused by the love of God. What's more, he has fallen in love afresh with his wife, a wonderful and unexpected blessing.

EIGHT

Loneliness

THE STATE OF BEING CHEERLESSLY SOLITARY—that's how Webster defines loneliness. Cheerlessly solitary. That may be the glummest definition in the entire dictionary. People just were not made to be alone, so involuntary solitude is a most unhappy state. It hurts to be lonely.

Many people in our modern society are lonely. At one time or another, you and I may count ourselves among them. In a summary of research on loneliness, *Psychology Today* identified two major kinds: situational loneliness and chronic loneliness. Situational loneliness stems from a significant event, often a change with social consequences, like a death, divorce, or a move to another part of the country. Chronic loneliness is a persistent emotional disorder which may or may not have its roots in some event but which lingers on indefinitely.

Loneliness is one of the social by-products of our industrialized culture. That's not to say people never experienced hurt over being alone in earlier times, because they did. However, it's safe to say that loneliness is more acute now than ever before.

Isolation has become a normal feature of our technological society. Increasingly we have tended to value people less for who they are than for what they can do. We forget the person and look to their usefulness. Treated this way, people can be shunted off into little compartments and there forgotten or ignored.

The fact is that at present more people are actually alone. Statistics drive the point home. On the basis of a survey of a cross section of the population, one sociologist estimates that between fifty and sixty million Americans feel extremely lonely at some time during any given month.

We live in a time of aggressive social decomposition. Relationships seem to be made in order to be broken. For example, the U.S. divorce rate has tripled since 1958, while the marriage rate in 1979 was at its lowest in forty years. Divorce may resolve one set of problems for the unhappy spouses, but it almost always causes new ones. Divorced persons, for example, tend to feel lonely and to feel that they are failures at relationships. One condition feeds the other, so divorcees find it hard to break out of the loneliness trap because of their fear of starting new friendships.

The young children of divorced parents seem to be especially vulnerable to loneliness, according to one psychologist who says that they keep trying to bring about a reconciliation of their parents, an attempt which is doomed to failure. They are often victims of chronic loneliness.

America's growing number of homeless children is a related problem. An estimated one million children live on our city streets, from Boston to Los Angeles, without shelter, without food, without friends, and without hope. They sleep in parks and doorways and eat whatever they can scavenge. About one-third of these youngsters support themselves as child prostitutes.

The Feeling of Loneliness

You do not have to be isolated, however, to feel lonely. With little or no effort, even though you may be surrounded by a small army of people, you can feel as alone as you would on a deserted island. The feelings may have roots in the objective deeds of others. Everyone seems to be going out with someone else, except you. You feel rejected. When you speak, no one seems to listen to what you have to say. You feel ignored. Someone snubs you. You feel rejected.

So, loneliness has a large emotional component. It can be an emotional problem, even a serious one. Few things are as painful as hurt feelings. And loneliness can breed other emotional difficulties, making you bristle with anger or paralyzing you into a depression. How many shy, insecure people began their career of self-hatred in a bout of loneliness?

Chronic loneliness is disconnected from the circumstances which may have occasioned it. Those who feel lonely for long periods, with no apparent reason at hand, also feel hopeless. They blame themselves for their situation and have convinced themselves that they can do nothing to improve it.

The King or Queen of Hearts

Our popular culture makes loneliness worse by leading us to expect that a special relationship with a member of the opposite sex is the answer for all our needs. The inescapable message of the media is this: bliss comes when you find your King or Queen of Hearts.

No matter where they turn, lonely people bump into the notion that romance is where it's at. They seem to buy into it as the only solution for loneliness, no matter how ineffective it turns out to be. One survey of college students, for example, identified a set of chronically lonely men who felt that the only possible cure for their problem was a romantic liaison. They did not feel, however, that they would be too successful at it—another symptom of their loneliness.

The failure of the lonely to have a lover deflates them even more. Or they may be motivated to go after relationships which may or may not cure their state of being cheerlessly solitary. Lonely people who take comfort in a casual erotic relationship are usually damaged by the experience and left more chillingly alone when it's over. Today, even marriage is often not the answer. As the divorce statistics indicate, those who find lovers may not find lifelong companions.

Romantic love is good, and I would not want to see it subtracted from our human make-up. However, when all is said and done, while romance might bring temporary relief, it is just not strong enough to cure loneliness.

The flaw in romantic love that renders it ineffective in healing loneliness is its focus on the self. True, lovers are absorbed in each other, but will anyone deny the supreme self-gratification which is essential to romantic love?

Loneliness is at core an emotional difficulty which focuses you on yourself. Those who suspect love is the antidote for it are correct, but not a love which is so radically self-concerned as romance. The cure is a love that is radically committed to others.

Love's victory over loneliness is one theme of the award-winning film, *Places in the Heart*. The story is set in a small, Texas town during the depression. A young woman, recently widowed, is joined by a black man, forced by prejudice into drifting, and by a blind man who was rejected by his family. Individually, their circumstances were bad enough to doom them to a life of failure, pain, and loneliness. However, because of the lady's pluck, and one is led to suspect also by God's grace, the three are forged together in friendship. As the film unfolds, we watch them grow in love for one another. We see them take care of each other. We witness their commitment to each other. We cheer them as together they face harsh circumstances and win.

The film closes with a visual commentary from 1 Corinthians 13, one of the most extraordinary elements I have seen in contemporary secular cinema. After the final scene, the entire cast of characters is assembled in the local church for a communion service. Love has reconciled people who had hated each other, and they are united in the Lord's Supper. While the bread and wine are passed among them, the lector is reading, "If I give away all I have, and if I deliver my body to be burned, but have not love, I gain nothing. Love is patient and kind; love is not jealous or boastful; it is not arrogant or rude." The love that cures loneliness is made of this stuff.

Staying Power

This kind of love is called agape, charity, or simply Christian love. Unlike romantic love, Christian love does not depend upon attraction to others. This is not to say that Christian love is without feeling, for it is expressed with warmth and signs of affection.

Christian love is also stronger and more stable than romantic love. It does not fluctuate with your feelings. On the other hand, romantic love wanes, even evaporates, when one lover is in a bad mood or feels attracted to someone else. Christian love has staying power. It's there motivating loving behavior in us, no matter how low, how tired, or how bad we feel.

One of the best models of Christian love I can point to is Bruce Ritter, the Catholic priest who founded Covenant House over a decade ago to rescue children from the streets of New York City. Our heart goes out to these kids, but they are hard to love because they are hard to help. Thrust onto the streets at age thirteen or fourteen, they learn to survive by making pacts with evil. They radiate bitter insolence, which is the hard shell behind which they conceal their fear and vulnerability. Love for them motivated Ritter to leave his teaching post for the streets. And he still loves them.

He once gathered a dozen hopeless boys to offer them a chance for jobs, a place to live, and training—a chance for a future. He wrote about it in his monthly column:

> One by one the kids began to understand what was happening. I mean, it didn't start out that way, but it became clear what was really happening. They had been afraid to hope and now they were beginning to—they hadn't wanted to. They didn't want to but they couldn't help it.
>
> I almost lost it . . . when the words from a haunting song by a group called Foreigner drifted up to the top of my mind and flicked across the back of my eyes:
>
> I want to know where love is.
> I want you to show me.
> I want to feel where love is.
> I know you can show me. . . .
>
> A kid with an old-young face, a ravaged face, looked at me. Keep me in mind if you start this program, Bruce. . . .

The meeting ended at that point. I didn't make any effort to hide what I felt. They didn't either.

One by one as they left, the kids reached out to shake my hand—but it really was just so we could touch each other.[8]

Of the 70,000 children who pass through Covenant House in a year, only one-third leave the streets. The rest go back—to their pimps, to the gay bath houses, to loneliness, degradation and death. But Bruce Ritter and his staff have not flagged in their zeal to show them what love is.

Christian love like this is founded upon the example and teaching of Jesus. He commanded his followers to love one another, just as he loved them. Because of our thick heads and hard hearts, he did not stop at words, but he showed us what his brand of love involved. "Do you love your sister? Then wash her feet—care for her—just as I, the Lord, have served you. Do you love your brother? Then sacrifice your life—your interests, your leisure, your time, your money—just as I did for you." Thus, Christian love is made of the lumber of the cross.

NINE

Turning to Others through Love

JESUS' KIND OF LOVE is the antidote for loneliness because it is radically oriented to others. When you decide to serve someone else, all attention is drawn from yourself to their interests. Christian love persuades you to stop asking, "What's in it for me?" and to begin wondering, "What can I do for others?"

There is a lot of teaching afloat which suggests that you cannot love others until you love yourself. Maybe so, but I think that much of this popular advice boils down to a recommendation of self-indulgence. It tells you to pamper yourself and look out for number one, since nobody else will.

For a Christian, real self-love comes not from looking out for yourself but from paying less attention to yourself, so you can give more to those you love.

This is the great Christian paradox. Jesus said if you cling to your own life, you will lose it, but if you lose it to serve him and others, you will live forever. Christian love somehow increases when you give it away. So you really love yourself most when you are so preoccupied with taking care of those you love that you stop focusing on yourself. What you give is what you get.

The Impossibility of Christian Love

All this is nice in theory, you say, but how on earth is it possible? I don't quibble with this objection. Christian love seems to be humanly impossible. We know ourselves too well. We don't find it easy to be kind, patient, or generous, which are marks of Christian love. Sometimes we find their opposites irresistible. We may even indulge ourselves in downright meanness. Love, Paul says, is never jealous, but we are often jealous. He also says love always rejoices in the right, but at times we get a kick out of wrong, either our own or someone else's.

The truth is that Christian love is not humanly possible. Without aid from another source, Christian love is just another nice theory competing with many other nice theories. What changes Christian love from mere words into real life is our personal relationship with Jesus.

If Jesus Christ were merely another philosopher who had taught his followers about love and left it at that, we would remember him in our history books along with Socrates and Plato. He would mean to us about as much as Marcus Aurelius does. And except to a relatively small group of people, that philosopher-emperor does not mean very much. Jesus, however, was not mainly a lawgiver who set standards for our relationships nor mainly a teacher who showed us the nature of love. He is all this, and more. He is God himself who not only instructs us and commands us to love each other but who also personally comes to us to help us do it.

It's easy to fall into step with the drummer who taps out the message everywhere: "Wasn't Jesus a great teacher, just like other great teachers! Wasn't the Sermon on the Mount a high-minded way of life, exactly like other high-minded ways of life?" We must break the rhythm of this seductively deceptive beat with a shout: "No! Jesus is not the teacher of a way, he *is* the way."

One of the passages in Scripture which I keep coming back to occurs in John's Gospel when Jesus addresses his disciples and us for the last time before his death. He tells us that he will not leave us orphans. He promises he will come to live in us, and his Father will come too. He assures us that we will come to know him and love him in the same way that he and the Father know and love each other. He says we will be his intimate, personal friends.

In the book of Revelation, John presents this truth of our personal knowledge of Jesus in dramatic picture language. Set this scene in your mind's eye. You are at table, ready to begin eating alone. It has been a long, hard day. Indeed, it has been a long, hard week, month, year. You know you are hungry and thirsty, but the pain of loneliness dwarfs the pangs of hunger, so you scarcely feel them. You wish something would happen to break the never-ending cycle of your cheerless solitude, but you know the monotony must be eternal.

Then, Someone knocks at your door. He shouts through the open transom that he wants to come in and share your meal with you. He says he loves you and wants to stay with you, not just tonight but tomorrow and forever. He promises you will never be alone again. He says he is Jesus. He wants to know if you will invite him in. Will you?

Jesus never intended us to go it alone, implementing his command to love by our own willpower. He wants to be our constant companion. With his aid, we can be kind, patient, and generous. We can let go of jealousy and meanness in his presence. Jesus himself is the best medicine for loneliness.

Ruth's Story

"I suspect a ruptured aneurysm in one of the blood vessels at the base of her brain," said the doctor. "Debbie is too sick to be moved now, but if she should still be alive in forty-eight to seventy-two hours, we will want to take her to Kansas University Medical Center for surgery."

If she should still be alive. The words cut painfully into Ruth's heart. She felt faint. Only a few hours ago, her seventeen-year-old daughter had been perfectly healthy. She had collapsed during Sunday morning worship, and now she was in intensive care, attached to monitors and a respirator, her young life slipping away.

It was the beginning of a long, lonely winter for Ruth, in which the Lord himself would be her consolation.

Looking for a miraculous healing, Ruth prayed a prayer relinquishing her daughter to God. She felt some relief but was called back from the snack bar to be told that Debbie had suffered a cardiac arrest. "I'm afraid Debbie can't get well," said the doctor.

"Where's the victory in relinquishment now?" Ruth cried inwardly. As all hope for Debbie's healing evaporated, she looked desperately for the Lord's purpose in her daughter's imminent death.

Late into the night Ruth besieged God with prayer for Debbie. The Lord spoke to her in her heart, not of promises of healing but of consolation. Revelation 3:20 came to Ruth's mind with particular force: "Behold, I stand at the door and knock; if any one hears my voice and opens the door, I will come in to him and eat with him, and he with me."

She understood the Lord to be saying that Debbie would be with him. The passage stuck so firmly in Ruth's mind that she came to see it also as the Lord's promise to comfort her in the loneliness ahead.

Debbie died the next morning. The Lord seemed to be present in the room, calming Ruth and her husband.

Then came the lonely winter. Ruth was often angry and depressed. For a while, remorse compelled her to relive her pregnancy with Debbie, looking for a cause for the congenital defect in Debbie's ruptured blood vessel—a quest doomed to fail, but one Ruth felt compelled to make. But in the moments of anger and depression, of remorse and self-pity, the Lord found a way to encourage Ruth. The pain of loneliness was no less sharp. A trenchant sword, it cleaved her mother's heart. But during a year-and-a-half of grief, the Lord was with Ruth, encouraging her and relieving her gloom.

One day at the end of this period, the Holy Spirit, sometimes called the Comforter in Scripture, entered Ruth's life in a fuller way. She was listening to a cassette about being filled with the Holy Spirit, and his presence touched her in a transforming way. From that time Ruth has had an assurance that "God, in the person of his Spirit, had come to sup with me in a way I had never dreamed possible."[9]

Where on Earth?

I am not going to advise lonely people to look for a church or a Christian group that has an orientation to service, community relationships, and expressed Christian love. That's not a bad suggestion. In fact, it's a good one. But the lonely have heard that advice a thousand times before and have been frustrated in their failure to find one.

You should not be surprised to learn that people can be lonely even among the liveliest, most loving Christians. The reason the search for Christian love often fails is that the seeker is mainly looking for what's in it for him. The search is relentlessly self-centered and, therefore, doomed. Remember the principle: what you give is what you get.

Where on earth can you find Christian love? It begins with you, in your own heart. We get Christian love by reaching out to others in love. One of the most dramatic stories I know of the triumph of love over loneliness is the story of the friendship of Paul Scott and Bishop Fulton J. Sheen.[10]

Paul Scott's life was interrupted during his senior year in high school, and it would never be the same. This normal, healthy lad, who enjoyed dancing and sports, contracted leprosy, now known as Hansen's disease. He spent the next six years lonely and frightened, confined in a leprosarium at Carville, Louisiana.

Newly discovered sulfone drugs halted the disease, but not before Paul was disfigured beyond repair. His face was an ugly mask, he was blind in one eye; he limped; and he had only partial use of his hands. Paul was spared his life, but only to meet with walls of rejection. People stared at him in the street; old friends avoided him; his own parents could not bear his deformities.

Horrible depression impelled Paul to look for help in an unlikely place. Although not a Catholic, he sought an appointment with Bishop Fulton J. Sheen, who had visited Carville and who seemed like a compassionate man. A little to Paul's surprise, Bishop Sheen invited him to his office.

"I've come to you because I have no one else to turn to," Paul said. "I haven't a friend in the world."

"Well, now you have one," said the Bishop.[11] He meant what he said. He had Paul Scott as a dinner guest regularly. Bishop Sheen loved Paul in down-to-earth ways: he cut his food for him at table; the bishop helped him furnish his apartment and provided him with clothes and food. More than anything else, he accepted Paul so that Paul was able to accept himself. Sheen encouraged him to look for God's purpose in his life, orienting Paul to find ways of serving others even though he himself was disabled. Paul was able to volunteer many hours of service with a social agency that helps troubled people. The Bishop's love had turned loneliness away and had given a man without hope reason to live.

There is a twofold lesson in this story. The first is that there is hope for lonely people if they will begin to reach out to others. What overcame Paul Scott's loneliness? Three loves: the love of God, the love of the bishop, and the love Paul Scott showed in his service of others. The last love is very close to the first; and it is regenerative.

The second is a message to those of us who do not feel lonely. Bishop Sheen has given us an example we dare not ignore. Those spared the pain of loneliness have an opportunity and even an obligation to show Christian love to lonely people in their lives. We should include those who always seem to be left out. We should invite them to recreate or to work with us around the house. The cure for loneliness is active, healthy relationships.

Lonely people feel as though they are in a hole. They don't like being there, but they feel unable to climb out. The steps which promise relief from their problem, and ultimately lead to their healing, are the very things they simultaneously long for and abhor. Turning to others is the way to emotional health for lonely people.

Start with a few small steps. Is there another lonely person in your neighborhood? In your family? In your own home? Pay them a visit. When they speak, listen to them and respond kindly. Do something for them that you know they need, like offering an elderly person rides to the grocery store or to the doctor's office.

Look for the chance to take bigger steps. If the opportunity arises to get involved in some Christian service to others, take it. Perhaps a local alternatives-to-abortion center needs volunteers or a suicide hotline is looking for counselors. Or your local church might need someone to teach little children.

The bottom line is that Christian love is what you make of it. If you are lonely, the revolution must begin with you. Turn away from yourself to the very needy people around you. There's plenty of wood for your cross right there in your neighbors, relatives, children, and spouses. You will not be going it alone. Your constant Companion will see you through.

TEN

Low Self-Esteem

CHARLIE BROWN IN THE COMIC STRIP *PEANUTS* is one of America's most popular cartoon characters. Oblivious to our obvious affection for him, Charlie feels that nobody likes him very much. Is it any wonder? He is the outsider of his little group of friends, the brunt of jokes, and an object of criticism instead of the friend he'd like to be, showered with approval and encouragement.

Charlie Brown feels bad about himself. I think that is the reason we like him so much. We identify with him and his situation, since we often find ourselves feeling the same way. Most of us, at one time or another, have felt hurt, rejected, or insecure. Feeling bad about yourself is a common emotional difficulty which affects some occasionally and others chronically. The bad news is that low self-esteem is a fairly tricky problem to deal with. The good news is that it is a problem we can overcome.

We Don't Get No Respect

We live in the styrofoam age. When we're done with something, we're used to tossing it. We treat people that way, too. I just saw a poster, beautifully framed, on sale for

$80 at a local mall. You may be familiar with the picture, which shows a fancy car, the caption I "heart" NY, and a poor beggar, curled up and asleep in a trash barrel. That piece will be a conversation stopper in somebody's family room. Perhaps the conversation will touch on the real message of the poster—that our society is riddled with distorted values. We don't value people for who they are. If they seem to be useless, they get discarded.

Is it any wonder that people feel bad about themselves when we have so little esteem for one another? We all laugh when the comedian Rodney Dangerfield complains, "I don't get no respect!" We are amused because we recognize ourselves in the joke: we don't get no respect either. Just a few short decades ago men honored women by tipping their hats and holding doors for them. Such signs of respect would seem quaint in many present situations because the respect they signify simply is not there.

The absence of honor would be bad enough. What's worse is that hostility has volunteered to fill the vacuum. A friend of mine once held a door for a young lady who was carrying a heavy package. She went through the door, made an obscene gesture, and kicked him in the leg. A dramatic symbol of the hatred typical of our times. We have all felt it at one time or another.

Like the flu, low self-esteem is a disease we catch from others. We get it from their words. True, we fashion our own self-concept, but we tend to build it out of what people say to us and about us.

Because of the intimacy of the relationship, what parents say to their children is most important. A dad, for example, who always expresses his own frustration by calling his son a "dummy," a "clumsy nerd," or worse, will certainly provide a strong negative twist to the boy's self-image. He is training the son to believe that when he has an accident, it is due to his alleged inborn clumsiness. When he makes a mistake, the son's memory will play the tape that repeats shrilly, "You stupid thing! You never do anything right!" And he'll believe it, piling up the evidence against himself.

Take Jim, for example. As a boy he always wanted to play the violin. His parents grudgingly paid for his lessons. They let him know that they thought it was a waste of money because he "didn't have any talent" for violin. He is now an accomplished violinist in a small orchestra. But in those early years, when jobs were few and far between, he often thought his parents had been right. He had very little self-confidence and their criticalness was at its root.

We Don't Get No Affection, Either

Words we fail to say to one another also contribute to the problem. We seem to have a chilly spot inside which blocks our ability to express love for people close to us. Fathers especially seem unable to tell their children how much they love them. Speaking affectionately and embracing seems sentimental, weak, or unmanly, so they balk at it. In a recent television special about teenage suicide, for example, one victim recalled that she could never remember her dad (or her mother, for that matter) ever telling her that he loved her.

We don't get no encouragement, either. We don't seem to be able to tell others, especially family and friends, that they have done well at something, like preparing a fine meal or getting a good grade. Our clumsiness at expressing affection and praise may lead us to conceal our warm feelings in negative banter, as in the common exchanges of teenaged brothers and sisters. These "putdowns" are awkward attempts at affection, but the packaging carries barbs that damage the receiver. How do you think Mrs. Dangerfield feels when Rodney says, "Take my wife, . . . please!?"

The irony, of course, is that the same chilly spot which blocks our ability to show affection longs to be warmed itself. We were made that way. Honor, respect, encouragement, affection—all are qualities God intended to be a normal part of human relationships. When they are absent, or worse, when their opposites are substituted for them, people do not fare so well. Since modern relationships tend to be based more on feelings than on commitments, the problem intensifies. We hanker after the approval of others, but no one seems to notice us, let alone affirm us. We should not be surprised to learn that most people have some problem with feeling bad about themselves.

Symptoms

People who feel bad about themselves tend to react defensively when they are corrected or criticized. Internally, they may recognize that they did something wrong. However, externally they dig in and brace themselves for self-defense. "And why not," they think. "No one else ever takes my side. I am always wrong."

Grace, for example, was a member of the leaders' team for a neighborhood Bible study evangelism group. Her insecurity had prevented her from attempting anything like it before, but she took great personal satisfaction in the role. When it became clear to the team that Grace was in a little over her head, they kindly asked her to accept some lesser responsibility for the Bible study. Grace put up a fuss, feeling that she was being unduly criticized, although no one had spoken a critical word to her. Sadly, Grace's low self-esteem could not handle even the gentle effort to help her serve more effectively. She left not only the leaders' team but the neighborhood outreach as well. And she left angry, complaining about the leaders.

People like Grace find it just as hard to take praise as they do criticism. They believe that they are so bad that when another speaks well of them they cannot accept it as true. When complimented, for example, they tend to brush it off by saying something like, "It was nothing," or, "Mary really did most of the work."

This behavior can seem to be very "spiritual." Jason, for example, is a young man who is fighting a severe case of low self-esteem. He belongs to a church fellowship which has reached out to him warmly. When people at church simply thank him for something, Jason always responds by saying, "It's not me, it's Jesus who did it." Jason wants to say, "I'm really too rotten to do anything good. So if anything good comes about through me, it has to be the Holy Spirit's doing." Jason's spiritual talk may make him sound "holy," but really it's a signal of a problem and a cry for help. Someone should tell him to say "You're welcome" when he is thanked and "Thank you" when he is complimented.

People with low self-esteem tend to conceal the problem by thinking or behaving as though they were better than others. This is a defense mechanism. Because of the emotional difficulty, they "know-deep-down" that they are not better than anyone, but they act superior to cover up the "truth."

For example, when I was a teenager, there was nothing I wanted more than to succeed at sports. However, I was small, uncoordinated, and performed poorly in every event I tried. My failure hurt a lot, but I pretended not to care. I thrust myself into academics and public speaking, at which I excelled. I worked at giving the impression that somehow sports were beneath me, and this pose masked my disappointment with myself.

We say people who behave like this are conceited. The people who do it feel like they are being proud because they are claiming to be better than others when they know they really are not. In fact, they feel as though they are actually much worse. So people with low self-esteem often think that they have a problem with pride, which they confuse with the conceit they have adopted to hide feeling bad about themselves.

This is one of the reasons that getting free from low self-esteem is tricky. When we're guilty of pride, we can repent for it. Real pride is sin, and repentance is the right remedy. Conceit is a cover for insecurity. When insecure people mistake their conceit for pride and try to repent for it, they make matters worse. Repentence here results in getting down on themselves and merely magnifies the original problem.

False Humility

At the same time, people who feel bad about themselves tend to defend themselves by regarding their problem as a virtue. They misinterpret their feeling "low" as lowliness and are inclined to think of themselves as "humble." So with a little sleight of hand they can become comfortable with an emotional problem by believing that at least there is something virtuous in it.

This defense mechanism shows itself in people who are asked to do a service and refuse because they "are not good enough" to do it. Pastors often get this response when they ask someone to take responsibility for a Bible study or serve as a deacon. For example, fifteen years ago I was active in a prayer group. I had some obvious gifts for teaching and leading worship, but because I was battling my problem with low self-esteem, I felt that I should not be involved on the leaders' team. I spent the better part of a year on the edges of the group, refusing to exercise my gifts and feeling very humble about it.

This brand of humility is a counterfeit. True humility does not take its definition from how a person feels toward himself but rather from how he relates to others. A humble person is not one who is always down on himself, acknowledging that everyone he meets is somehow better than he. A person who thinks that way may be virtuous in many respects, but he also has an emotional difficulty.

Now you can see why overcoming low self-esteem can be tricky. If we deceive ourselves into believing that it is a virtue, we hang on to it and are not able to let it go.

ELEVEN

Forgiveness, Service, and Encouragement

SOMEONE ONCE SAID that acquiring self-confidence was like doing the cha-cha: one step forward, one step back, and three steps in the same place. That is an overly pessimistic view. Getting free of low self-esteem is more like three steps forward and one back. It is not easy, but with grace and effort we can make good progress.

Forgiveness. First, we have to remove internal blocks that stand in the way of overcoming the problem. The biggest of these by far is the hurt done to us by others. Bitterness is the best fertilizer to guarantee a bumper crop of low self-esteem.

Our hurt feelings are normally rooted in real injuries. If we are honest about it, we will admit that anger, and unsavory feelings like desire for revenge, magnify our pain. We ought to hope that someday people who harmed us will tell us that they are sorry for the damage. However, if we wait for that, we may simply be deciding to wallow in misery for a very long time.

The initiative is with us. We can begin by forgiving the

people who have injured us—the parents who never had a good word for us; the brother who always put us down; those who blackballed us from the in-group at school or work, and so on. These acts of forgiveness are acts of the heart. They normally do not involve speaking to the offenders directly unless they ask us to forgive them.

Helen's story is typical and instructive. She was the fourth child of parents who had planned to have three children. Helen's mother resented having to abandon her plans of a career in order to care for the newcomer, a fact which marred their relationship. The mother always made Helen feel unwanted. When anything went wrong and tension mounted, Helen was told that things were going bad because of her. For twenty years Helen was made to feel that everyone would have been better off if she had never been born.

When Helen got help as a young adult, the Christian woman who counseled her persuaded her that first she must forgive her mother. This was very hard because, as Helen explained, she did not feel very forgiving toward her mother. "I am not asking you to feel forgiving toward your Mom," said the counselor wisely, "and I'm not suggesting that you even have any good feelings about her. I am just asking you to decide in your heart to say, 'I forgive my mother.' The Lord will help you. And in time, maybe sooner than you expect, your feelings toward her will improve."

Helen did her best to take the advice. Things went as the counselor had predicted. Helen forgave her mother and holds no grudges, even though they still do not have a close personal relationship. But once Helen had forgiven the person who hurt her most, she began to win her battle with low self-esteem. Occasionally she still has a little bout with insecurity, but most of her friends regard her as self-confident and even-tempered. Three steps forward, one back.

When the Lord taught us to pray, he said pray like this: forgive us our sins as we forgive those who have sinned against us. We take far too casual an attitude toward the Lord's Prayer. In the first part, the Lord has us pray that we obey the Father's will just as it is obeyed in heaven, which is perfectly. A worthy prayer, but one we find hard to live out, since perfect obedience to God contradicts our evil tendencies. In the latter part of the prayer, the Lord has us make a contract with the Father to the effect that he should measure out his forgiveness for us just as generously as we measure out forgiveness to those who offend us. Or just as miserly.

The Lord's Prayer pledges us to be the first to forgive and to forgive unconditionally. It should not be, "I'll forgive them, if they do this or that," but simply, "I forgive." That seems hard because when we are offended or injured, our feelings get hurt. They are often so deeply wounded that they obstruct more important healings—the repairing of broken relationships. However, forgiveness is the Lord's idea. He will help us even when we don't feel like forgiving. If we practice forgiveness, our relationships will be healthier, and we will have a firmer basis on which to build our self-confidence. Forgiveness works against low self-esteem.

Service. People who feel bad about themselves are easy prey for self-centeredness. When we are hurt, we let our minds dwell on it. If we feel rejected, we tend to feel sorry for ourselves. We investigate within to see if we really are as bad as people seem to say we are. Introspection becomes our defense as we analyze our feelings and our motives so we can justify our behavior. We feel bad about ourself, but it's all we have, so we focus on it. We would bristle with rage if someone said we were "self-centered" or "selfish," but these would be accurate words to describe our condition.

Scripture understands this tendency and the evils it leads to. The biblical antidote for it is humility. A humble person takes the attitude of one who serves. He makes it a goal in life to care for the needs of others. The apostle Paul, for example, says the humble person "looks not only to his own interests but also the interests of others" (Phil 2:4), and he presents Jesus' giving up his life for us as the ultimate model of humility.

Low self-esteem bends our mind's eye inward towards the self. Humility turns it outward to others. This is profound biblical teaching on the healing of emotional disorders. Practically speaking, this means looking around for someone who has a need and finding some way to help them. Generously serving someone else helps us make giant strides toward our own emotional health. "It seems too simple," you say? Yes, it is simple. The deepest truths about living are that way.

When we stop being preoccupied with our own difficulties and turn our attention from ourselves to others, we are giving ourselves a chance to heal within. It's not just that shouldering another's burden may make ours seem lighter. A sore heals more quickly if we stop scratching the scab. When we stop fussing about our problems, we give the Holy Spirit a chance to heal us.

Let me tell you how I was cured of a long-standing bout with self-hatred. Just after I realized how foolish I had been to refuse to serve in a prayer group out of a false sense of humility, I plunged into working with a group closer to my home. Daily for about seven years, the needs of others came ahead of, or at least had equal time with, my own. I shared overall concern for the group with several other men and women. Welcoming people to the group; helping meet their needs; leading them to a personal relationship with Jesus; giving teachings; leading prayer meetings; giving counsel; and providing many other services ended up benefitting me as much as the group.

It was a healing process. Gradually, self-respect and self-confidence came to replace condemnation and insecurity. Humility—that is, losing myself in generous service of others—occasioned my getting free from low self-esteem. One of my closest friends, commenting on the difference in me now, suggests with a wink that I may have over-corrected, just a little.

Encouragement. About six years ago I met a young black man at a men's evangelistic breakfast. He was obviously intrigued by the group, but he was reserved and a bit suspicious. I got to know James well over the next several years. He was a younger member of a large, lower middle-class family from a large city. The family had endured many problems, crowned by the parents' recent divorce. James distanced himself from his insecurity by adopting many different poses which he himself called masks.

We became close friends. In the course of many conversations, it became clear to me that my very positive evaluation of this fine young man clashed harshly with his equally negative self-view. My heart's desire for him was that somehow he could come to see himself as I did.

I spent a good bit of time in the first years of our friendship simply giving James encouragement. He might tell me about some difficulty he had at school or work, blaming or belittling himself. I tried to give him a more objective perspective. Often I would help him pick out his strong points, especially those that stood out in situations he found hard. I praised him for achievements every chance I got. I am sure James could feel it in his bones that I loved him. That helped him very much.

It wasn't easy for James to take praise because he believed the bad feelings he had about himself. One day I told him a story that had helped me. Bob Mumford says he used to feel guilty when people came to the podium to praise him for having given an inspiring talk. He was afraid it would go to his head and he would commit the sin of pride. Then Mumford realized that his teaching was his service in the body of Christ. While God could inspire others through him, it was Bob Mumford's wit and speech that reached them. He felt God wanted him to draw into himself whatever praise people gave him, somewhat like taking in a great breath. Then, at night, he would give all the praise to God, exhaling all he had taken in.

James was persuaded. He more readily welcomed my positive input. Slowly he began to take a better view of himself. I noticed as we visited that he was more and more positive about himself. I also observed that we came to talk more about topics other than James' problems, a sign of his growth in humility.

If you were to meet James today, I doubt you would pick up whatever traces of the problem that may linger. The encouragement he got from me, and from many others, built his self-confidence and banished his self-hatred.

The Holy Spirit

Forgiveness, true humility, and encouragement are all agents which can help free us from low self-esteem. The real source of our freedom, however, is the Holy Spirit. The Lord gave him to us as a gift, a foretaste of eternal life, and a down payment on our heavenly inheritance. Just as words from people can give us a twisted view of ourselves, words from God who dwells in us can straighten us out. The Holy Spirit assures us of our Father's love for us. If he's for us, who can be against us? And he is for us. If you have a problem with low self-esteem, let your road to recovery begin with turning yourself over more completely to the Holy Spirit. You cannot put yourself into better hands.

TWELVE

Worry

"WHAT'S ON YOUR MIND, STEPHEN?" My wife, Mary Lou, had noticed that Stephen, one of our more serious offspring, was sulking around her kitchen. He wanted to talk about something but did not know how to start. "Something must be bothering you, son. What is it?" she asked.

"Well, Mom," Stephen said, shifting his scant fifty pounds from one foot to the other. "I have been wondering about something. It may sound funny to you. I'm not sure I want to say it."

"C'mon, Stephen. You can ask me. Even if it's funny to me, I promise I won't laugh," she nudged him on. I wonder how many times Mary Lou has regretted making such vain promises!

"Well, uh," he stammered. "Is, uh, Daddy, uh . . . a full grown man?"

I don't know how Mary Lou restrained herself from bursting into laughter. "Of course, Stephen, your Dad is a full grown man! He may be getting wider, but he stopped getting taller twenty years ago," she chuckled.

My little boy ran from the room in tears, crying, "Oh, no! I'll never get very big!"

Stephen had been indulging in one of America's favorite pastimes—worry. We worry about everything. Like my son, we worry over things we cannot possibly change or avoid—everything from our height to our death. We may even worry about life in general. An older man I know was once asked what he was going to do upon his retirement. The elderly man responded, "Pursue my favorite pastime—'viewing with alarm.'"

Worry is a form of fear. It encompasses both specific fears and that vague yet painful free-floating fear which we sometimes call anxiety. Worry can be a big and chronic problem. Worried people are unhappy people. They become preoccupied with feelings of fear, turning in on themselves and filling up with self-concern.

Have you noticed how worry tends to immobilize people? For example, I know several people who are so anxious about what others think of them that they have reduced their social contacts to a bare minimum. Worry about some serious problem, like a son or daughter in trouble, can make a parent physically ill or emotionally unstable. Worry and the problems that come with it can mess us up quite a bit.

When Worry Is Good

Worry, however, is not always bad. When worry is an expression of concern, it may be constructive. This is normally the case only when we have responsibility for, or the capacity to do something about, the thing that worries us. Suppose you notice that money is frequently missing from your purse or pocket. You grow concerned that one of your children may be stealing from you. If your worry about the child provokes you to help him, then it is good. If, however, you let the worry eat at you and you take no appropriate steps in response, it is harmful because it damages you and has no positive effect.

Most of the time worry is not good. We tangle ourselves up with fears about matters over which we have no control nor any ability to influence personally. Grief-stricken parents stand by helplessly as the marriages of their children crash on the rocks of divorce. The parents have tried everything—urging counseling, sending clergymen, arguing, manipulating, pleading, praying—to no avail. Once the point of no return has been reached, worry can no longer be helpful. If there is nothing more we can do to change a bad situation, worry ceases to be of any use because it is only good as a motivator to prevent something undesirable. In cases like this, all worry can do is hurt the worrier.

Where Worry Comes From

Worry is a fear reaction which is standard operating equipment in human beings. The most common sources of worry are intimately experienced dangers, no matter how remote they may actually be. In a recent survey of 1,000 readers, for example, *Psychology Today* discovered the not-so-surprising fact that the top three fears of respondents were the loss of a loved one, serious illness, and financial disaster (tied with nuclear war). People tend to worry most about those things that hit them right at home. That's always been the case.

If people today worry more than their ancestors—and I think we do—the sources are our increasing need for social approval and the effect of broken relationships.

People today tend to be emotionally fragile, extremely vulnerable to what other people may think of them. We have our receivers tuned in to the approval signals transmitted by our peers. Does he like me? Does she think I'm too fat? Too thin? Too tall? Will the people at my new job accept me? Maybe there is something about me they won't like and they'll avoid me. The cartoonist Larson captured the spirit of this fear in *The Far Side*, when a lady dragon turns her back on her would-be lover dragon, saying, "Larry, it's not you, it's just your breath. It's so fresh and minty."

When society is stable and relationships are working right, people feel more secure. They experience themselves as valued for who they are. They sense that they fit in, so they do not need to seek approval. But ours is a disintegrating society. Some even use stronger language. They say our society is "atomized"; that is, people have no significant relationships and are so isolated that they must look after themselves. They may live among crowds of people but they are really alone. In this context, how others regard us matters a lot.

For example, the mobility of our society has scattered families all over the map. My mother's brothers and sisters lived their entire lives within five miles of each other. When there was a need in our family, aunts and uncles swarmed in with help. That doesn't happen much any more, mainly because the job market disperses us. And the more alone we are, the more prone we are to anxiety.

Worry also increases in direct proportion to the brokenness of relationships. Divorce has become commonplace throughout the western world. Love has been twisted into hate everywhere. In California, for example, there is the incredible phenomenon of children of divorced parents having to lobby to compel their dads to pay their child support. The victims of broken commitments have a lot to worry about. They have been forced to look out for themselves. They worry because they feel that they will sink under the weight of their troubles.

Assert Yourself

"Don't just lay there like a doormat, wallowing in worries. Get up! Assert yourself. Do something about it! Nobody else is going to do it for you!" This is the self-help advice which the pop-psychology industry directs to worriers. Once you get past the junk, there is a kernel of wisdom to be found there.

There is good advice to be found, for example, in the assertiveness training movement. But you must handle with care, separating the wheat from the chaff. When Frank, of the Frank and Ernest comic strip, goes to sign up for assertiveness training, he says, "Now I don't want too much. Just enough so I don't have to inherit the earth."

Frank misunderstands meekness here. Like many of us, he thinks that being meek means being a milquetoast. The brand of meekness which enables us to inherit the earth, according to the Sermon on the Mount, does not mean passively enduring everything that comes our way. Real meekness is Christian love in action. It refers to having a heart to serve others, being generous to others, and putting our own interests last.

Nowhere does Jesus teach that meekness excludes firmness. We are supposed to be meek in our relationships and simultaneously stand up for what is right. Meekness and assertiveness are good companions, with meekness predominating. So, we can learn from the self-help programs as long as we judge our behavior by Christian standards.

The nugget of good advice in assertiveness training is the value of "fight." Christians sometimes disagree over whether or not it's right to engage in fighting which inflicts injury on other people. That's not my subject here, so I think I can safely skirt the issue. The kind of fight I mean is the mental battle we must wage against thoughts or feelings which would numb us with fear.

Fight is one of the main resources we have for combating worry and anxiety. When something troubles us, we can let worry engulf our minds and give it control over our behavior. Or we can fight it. We can assert ourselves against worry and maintain our ability to act confidently.

Face the Worry Squarely

I'd like you to meet my friend, the "What If?" Lady. Perhaps you know someone like her. She always wonders what will happen if she comes down with cancer, if her house burns down tomorrow, if social security collapses before she dies, and so on. There is hardly any correlation between her worries and her actual situation. When asked, she can point to no fact which might give reason for her worry. Nothing but subjective fears—very real fears, mind you—but without objective foundations.

People like the "What If?" Lady must fight. They would be wise to regard their minds as a battlefield on which a victory has been won. They should think of themselves as captains assigned to hold the ground that has been taken. The weapon they fight with is simply the truth. When an irrational fear pops up, they must confront it. "What if I get cancer?" worry asks. The truth answers, "Well, right now I am healthy. I don't smoke. No one in my family ever had cancer. I don't think I need to worry about that." If we fill our minds with truths, we make irrational fears unwelcome.

Several years ago, when I was involved in campus ministry, I was asked to give a talk at a parents' meeting. My colleagues had prepared an outline for my presentation based on their experience with similar meetings. I was supposed to correct the parents for manipulating their children and for refusing to forgive them.

I worried a great deal about that talk. Many of the parents were twenty years my senior. I was afraid to tell them they were relating poorly to their children. Why wouldn't they say, with some accuracy, that this young man is "wet behind the ears?" Why wouldn't they object that I had no experience and shouldn't be telling them what to do?

The mental game I was playing here is called rationalization. I was inventing reasons to justify my feelings of fear. I remember standing before that group of parents, quivering with worry just before I was about to address them. I recall deciding to drive the fearful thoughts from my mind. I told myself that these good people would appreciate hearing helpful Christian truths. So I gave the talk with some measure of confidence. Do you know what? The parents loved it. Many came forward to thank me for it.

Fighting worry involves mental discipline. We must learn to recognize the stream of negative feelings and thoughts at their source and refuse to embrace them. We should not make worries feel at home in our minds by inventing reasons to support them.

We can fight worry better if we have someone to talk to about the things that bother us. We can become so good at rationalizing fears that the truth itself appears to be unreasonable and false. A friend who listens to our concerns and who evaluates the situation for us can help get us in position to fight. He or she can tell us the truths we need to oppose the fears. Sam, a young friend of mine, is a case in point. Sam is a likable and friendly man who, however, used to see himself as inept in social settings. His job required him to be in constant direct contact with people. He worried so much about how well he was relating to his clients that it made him ill on occasion.

Sam and I had a man-to-man talk about his worry. I gave him a frank evaluation of his ability to interact socially and of his faulty perceptions about himself. Armed with a true view of himself, Sam was gradually able to relate more confidently and without anxiety.

The examples I have given are trifles compared to the worries which plague us. Alcoholism, disease, unemployment, divorce, and the like generate a high degree of anxiety. While these problems are bigger, however, the same principle works to combat the worries they produce. We have the choice of letting worry incapacitate us, paralyzing us so that we can barely respond to the challenge that problems present. Or we can fight worry with truth so that we can live effectively amid the worst of circumstances.

Mental discipline can keep worry under control, but it cannot diffuse it completely. The real antidote for worry is faith in God. If worry drives us into his arms, it can be an occasion of our growing in strength.

THIRTEEN

Turning to God in Faith

ONE OF MY FAVORITE STORIES in the Old Testament is about Gehazi, the young servant of the prophet Elisha (see 2 Kgs 6). With a name like that, I sometimes wonder if he was a distant relative of mine.

Once when the King of Syria was preparing secret military moves against Israel, Elisha was able to keep his own king informed of the enemy plans through prophecy. Frustrated by the prophet's gift, the Syrian monarch sent a vast army to silence him.

When Gehazi saw the Syrian warriors, horses, and chariots, he was overwhelmed with fear. Here I note a family resemblance beyond the similarity in our names, since I too find that threatening circumstances push my panic button.

Elisha came out to survey the army amassed against him. We would expect him to run back inside, trying to find a way to escape unseen. Instead, Elisha encouraged Gehazi: "Fear not, for those who are with us are more than those who are with them" (2 Kgs 6:16). Then the prophet prayed that God would give his servant the spiritual eyes to see that the nearby mountain was occupied by a mighty spiritual army, far bigger than the Syrian force.

Too often, we are more like Gehazi than Elisha. We come up against obstacles in our life, and we are overcome by anxiety. We often behave as though we believe that reality is strictly three dimensional. We too readily accept the lie that "what you see is what you get." Or we are too quick to agree with Henry Ford, who said, "History is one damned thing after another," or with Dorothy Parker, who said, "No, Mr. Ford, history is the same damned thing over again." In short, we fail to look beyond.

Faith Is the Key

If we want to win over worry, we must become more like Elisha. He was a man of faith. He knew that God was more powerful than the King of Syria, and he trusted God to deliver him. By faith, Elisha singlehandedly delivered the entire Syrian army into the hands of the King of Israel, putting an end to that threat.

The trouble with stories like this one is that instead of inspiring us to greater faith they can leave us discouraged. We feel that we are more like Gehazi and are unable to see ourselves in Elisha's shoes. We think we will never have enough faith, so why bother. This view misunderstands faith.

Faith is not a source of spiritual energy. It is merely the switch that gives access to spiritual power, or better, the key which opens the door through which grace flows. We don't have to generate spiritual power on our own, which we are often tempted to try. We don't even have to possess the personal strength to break down the door. We need only turn the key by resting our faith on God.

We have all seen beginning swimmers thrashing around in the water, struggling to stay afloat. The more they kick and splash, the more they sink. Then the instructor tells them to relax, lean back, and let the water hold them up. As they calm down and rest in the water, they discover that the water itself buoys them up. Faith is like that. We rest in God who loves us, and his power works to bring us through today's trials.

When Jesus commands us to trust God and orders us not to worry, he is offering help, not condemnation. "Therefore, I tell you, do not be anxious about your life, what you shall eat, nor about your body, what you shall put on.... Which of you by being anxious can add a cubit to his span of life? If then you are not able to do as small a thing as that, why are you so anxious about the rest? ... And do not seek what you are to eat and what you are to drink, nor be of anxious mind. For all the nations of the world seek these things; and your Father knows that you need them. Instead, seek his kingdom, and these things shall be yours as well" (Lk 12:22, 25-26, 29-32).

Here Jesus tells us to put an end to worry by making a big switch in attitude. We must, he says, stop depending on ourselves and depend on God to take care of us. That's a tall order, or at least it seems so. We are so accustomed to doing things for ourselves, we have little experience of being cared for, even by God. But Scripture tells us that God loves us. When you get right down to it, if he didn't provide for us, we would really have something to worry about. There would actually be no way out for us. We would be simply doomed.

The key to leaving worry behind and receiving mercy from God consists of a straightforward decision to want God's kingdom more than anything else. That's what we say every time we pray the prayer Jesus taught us. What else are we saying when we pray, "Our Father... Your kingdom come, your will be done, on earth as it is in heaven?" We are inviting God to rule in our lives. We are renouncing the "Burger King" principle that reigns in America and confessing our trust and obedience to God: we are saying we no longer "want it our way" but desire more than anything to live our lives on God's terms.

My wife, Mary Lou, made a decision like that twenty-five years ago. Together we are in the process of raising seven children. You will believe me when I say that we have had our worries. We have also seen the Lord work when we have trusted him.

For example, four years ago, Mary Lou was anxious about her parents. Her father was about to die, and it was not clear that he had everything right with God. In addition, Mary Lou worried about what would happen to her mother. How could she manage the big two-story house on the Pittsburgh hillside?

So the Ghezzi family prayed every day for many months. The children especially asked the Lord for a happy death for Grandpa. The prayer was answered. My father-in-law died reconciled to God. We continued to pray for Grandma, expecting the Lord to show his care. In a short time, my mother-in-law was persuaded to sell her home of twenty-five years and move to a first-floor apartment near shops and church.

So that I don't make it sound too easy, let me make a disclaimer. Faith is not a magic wand that we can wave to get whatever we want. That's because we cannot tell God what to do and what not to do. God is not our servant. He is the Lord. Faith is the right attitude for us to have toward him. When we ask for something, sometimes the answer is yes. Sometimes, however, he says wait, or no. Faith does not direct God but receives from him. Faith says with the saints,

"Grant that I might love you always, then do with me what you will."

Nor will I be absolutely free of the feelings of fear when I exercise my faith. I am reminded of another story about Mother Angelica. She takes Maalox for upset stomach. One day someone asked her why she had to take stomach medicine if she had faith. Mother Angelica responded, "Oh, I have faith, but my tummy doesn't know it yet." If we want it God's way and are trusting him, so what if our stomach flutters a little or if a twinge of fear passes through our brain? God does not scrutinize us for imperfections before he gives us mercy; he gives us mercy to free us of imperfections.

Worrying Our Way to Confidence

If worry occasions our growth in faith, for all its bad, discomforting side effects, it will have done us a great good. Faith may enable us to worry our way to confidence, thus transforming a spiritual debit into an asset.

My favorite children's story makes the point unforgettably. It is the tale of Dooley and the Snarly-Snort-Snoot. Dooley was a thirteen-year-old giant, the son of enormous parents. However, Dooley had never grown. He was about the same size as ordinary thirteen-year-old children. His mother worried about him. Hoping to trigger a growth spurt, she always nagged him to eat everything on his plate. His father just seemed to wait patiently for things to change.

Dooley worried about his size, too. Occasionally he would try to frighten the local children, but they usually turned the trick and terrorized him.

One day a Snarly-Snort-Snoot, an incredibly vicious

monster, came to the village. This ferocious beast was really something to worry about. He surveyed the scene and decided to devour Tricia, who happened to be Dooley's girlfriend. Alarmed, Dooley forgot himself and jumped with both feet on the beast's armored tail. The irritated Snort-Snoot took one look at Dooley, sized him up as a bigger lunch, and began to chase him.

Dooley ran about fifty feet. Then something clicked in his mind, and he stopped suddenly. "Wait a minute," he said to himself, "I'm a giant and giants don't run." So he turned, faced the monster, and shouted a giant's challenge: "Fee! Fie! Foe! Fum!" Immediately, Dooley grew two feet taller. This performance halted the startled beast momentarily, but he soon resumed the chase, his appetite whetted by Dooley's unexpected increase in size.

Fifty feet further down the road, Dooley again confronted the Snort-Snoot. The effect was the same: Dooley shot up two more feet, and the monster came after him all the more eagerly. However, the third challenge was a turning point for Dooley. As he roared, "Fee! Fie! Foe! Fum!" Dooley assumed his full giant size. The Snort-Snoot cowered before him and fled, wimpering like a spanked puppy.

I am attracted to Dooley because I see something of myself in him. When I forget who I am, fear and anxiety can immobilize me. Then the Snarly-Snort-Snoots of every day can wreak havoc in my life. However, when I remember that I am a Christian, the son of a mighty Father, I can behave confidently. Faith in God makes me stand tall in the face of trouble, and I can send the Snort-Snoots off squealing with their tails between their legs.

Worries, like swarms of locusts, can consume all that is wholesome in our lives. Excellent men and women regularly succumb to them, devastated by their fearsome attacks. For those who fight and have faith, however, the same horde of fears and anxieties can be opportunities for courageous action. Like other problems, worry can be a turning point for faithful men and women, an opportunity to become more like Jesus.

FOURTEEN

Becoming More Like Jesus

Humpty Dumpty sat on a wall,
  Humpty Dumpty had a great fall.
All the King's horses and all the King's men,
  Couldn't put Humpty Dumpty together again.

PERSONAL PROBLEMS CAN LEAVE US FEELING like poor old Humpty Dumpty. They may break us down so completely that we think we can never be restored to our former selves. That can be bad if the problems do damage which seems to be beyond repair, like the recurring insecurity that comes from years of low self-esteem. However, if the problem provokes changes in parts of our character which were contrary to Christ, then there's a chance that we will be the better for it. For example, a severe bout with despair can be a turning point for a person prone to hopelessness, if at last he places trust in God.

Problems, like coins, have two sides. One side, which in slang is called "tails," represents the evil we are suffering. The other, called "heads," represents the strength God wants to produce in us. For example, when we are racked by despair, we are viewing the reverse side of a problem, the obverse of which is trust in God. This analogy with coins suggests that we value our problems and that we regard them with thanksgiving. A silver dollar has the same value whether we are looking at "heads" or "tails." A problem also has value for us, but we are going to have to turn it over from "tails" to "heads" to appreciate it. For example, we must see that despair invites us to hope before we can be very thankful for our desperate condition.

Problems make us malleable in areas of weakness, and the love of God works there to build us up, reproducing the strengths which characterize Jesus. By the power of the Holy Spirit, he imprints the image of Christ in us, as the image of a celebrated person is stamped on a coin. Thus, the Lord uses our problems to make us more like Christ.

As despair opens us to trust, other problems can be chances for us to grow in specific character traits of Jesus. The following list shows which marks of Christ correspond to the problems dealt with in this book.

Guilt — Peace
Disappointment — Hope
Lust, Greed, Envy — Self-control, Chastity
Loneliness — Love, Mercy
Low Self-Esteem — Humility, Confidence
Worry — Faith

I used disappointment and hope as illustrations above. Let's review the other sets of problems and the Christian virtues they can occasion.

Guilt — Peace. We suffer from guilt when we have broken our relationship with God and with others. We feel this alienation deeply; it is like a spiritual worm gnawing at our heart. The love of God invites us to repent for sin and to restore relationships with those whom we have injured or who have harmed us.

Peace is the mark of Christ which grows in us when we come back to a right relationship with God. "Let the peace of Christ rule in your hearts, to which indeed you were called in the one body," wrote Paul (Col 3:15). Peace is a spiritual conduit which enables the love of God to electrify us. Peace also refers to the activity of maintaining healthy relationships among members of the body of Christ. In particular, we are marked by peace when we harmonize disagreements and put an end to fighting. Jesus said, "Blessed are the peacemakers, for they shall be called sons of God" (Mt 5:9).

Disorderly desires — Self-control. A person who has triumphed over lust or greed will have grown in the Christian virtue which Scripture describes as self-control. Paul says, "The fruit of the Spirit is ... self-control," which he presents as the obverse of wicked behavior like impurity, envy, and carousing (Gal 5:23).

As we turn from disorderly desires back to God, we will be more in control of our selves. Our wills will be strengthened for resisting temptation. But our self-control will not simply be a victory of our own willpower. Real self-control is primarily the triumph of the love of God in us. Fulton Sheen tells the following story which illustrates the point:

> There was a priest who had a high office in one diocese. He was removed from office because of alcoholism. He went to another diocese but continued to give scandal. He happened to come into a retreat when I was talking about taking a regular hour for personal prayer, and he

made the "holy hour" from that time on. He died in the presence of the Lord a month or two later. He had been battling drunkenness for years. But he overcame it in the end because of the expulsive power of the new affection. He fell in love with the Lord.[12]

Sheen asks, "How do we get rid of evil? By the expulsive power of a new affection. We do not drive out evil, rather we crowd it out.... We crowd it out when we bring something else in. It's like a man who leads an evil life until he meets a fine woman who leads him in the path of virtue."[13] We have self-control when there is so much love for God in our hearts that there is no longer any room for anything else. Then the love of God robs lustful or envious images of their seductiveness, and we have the freedom to ignore them. Jesus said, "Blessed are the pure in heart, for they shall see God" (Mt 5:8).

Loneliness — Mercy. Jesus was lonely. John says, "He came to his own home, and his own people received him not" (1:11). Before he had completed his mission, even his closest companions had rejected him. Yet loneliness did not imprison him in isolation, for he reached out to all who came: to the blind, the adulterers, the possessed, the lonely. Mercy is that mark of Jesus which describes his willingness to give aid where he saw a need. Lonely people ought to let themselves fall so much in love with Jesus that they allow him to move them out of themselves towards others. Jesus said, "Blessed are the merciful, for they shall obtain mercy" (Mt 5:7).

Low self-esteem — Humility. The other side of low self-esteem is self-confidence, and the way to get there is humility. However, the path to deliverance from this problem takes us through a jungle inhabited by self-hatred, condemnation, self-pity, and other wild beasts, and getting to a clearing is not easy.

Humility is one of the more misunderstood marks of Jesus and is often falsely identified with self-abasement, or even belittling oneself, which itself is low self-esteem. As we saw in chapters 5 and 11, humility means having an accurate assessment of yourself and assuming an attitude of service to the Lord. The Bible describes Jesus as meek and humble of heart, which means he knew who he was and had placed himself in his Father's service and in the service of God's people. Confidence comes when the love of God frees us to imitate Jesus, who came as one who serves.

Worry — Faith. Worry is the seedbed for faith, which will grow luxuriantly in us like a tropical plant that germinates and grows overnight, if we'll let it. Worry is a kind of spiritual fussiness which intrudes our concerns into situations, shutting out God's initiatives. The worrier must shift from depending upon himself to relying on God, a switch which he understands rationally but which emotionally and psychologically he finds hard to make. Worry produces faith when we respond to God's love and relax in his care. Remember, growing in faith is like learning to swim. Faith will buoy us up if we rest in it. But we won't have the chance to grow if we stand on the edge of the pool, worrying about ourselves. The Lord seems to be saying, "Come on in, the water's fine."

Viewing problems as opportunities for growing more like Christ is seeing them with God's eyes. His vision penetrates us, and he knows our sins and weaknesses. He brings us to crises—turning points—so that his love can cleanse us, rebuild a broken part here, replace a rotten section there, and finally bring us to freedom and maturity as his sons and daughters.

Once when I was suffering from problems, a friend of mine wrote me a note to remind me of how relentless God's love for me is. He said, "You can run in the creek to leave no scent; you can go back over your backtrack; you can tiptoe along the top of every rail fence in the county; but you cannot throw the hound of heaven off your trail. I'm sure he is about to overtake you with big changes in areas that have long resisted salvation." Let's all stop running and let him catch us.

Notes

1. Lillian Butler, "Mary's Secret," *New Covenant* 11, no. 8 (February 1982): 32.
2. Francois Mauriac, *Knot of Vipers*, from *A Mauriac Reader* (New York: Farrar, Straus and Giroux, 1968), 391.
3. Ibid., 354.
4. Ibid., 419.
5. Ibid., 423.
6. "The War Within: An Anatomy of Lust," *Leadership* III, no. 4 (Fall 1982): 43.
7. Ibid., 45.
8. Bruce Ritter, "Hope Resurfaced—Lives Regained," *Our Sunday Visitor* 74, no. 2 (May 12, 1985): 14.
9. Ruth VanArsdale, "The Long Winter," *New Covenant* 11, no. 1 (July 1981): 12.
10. Paul Scott, "The Friendship," *The Guideposts Treasury of Love* (New York: Bantam, 1982), 260.
11. Ibid., 261.
12. Fulton J. Sheen, *Through The Year With Fulton Sheen* (Ann Arbor: Servant Books, 1985), 15.
13. Ibid., 14.

Other Books of Interest from Servant Publications

The Angry Christian
Bert Ghezzi

With ample illustrations of how the angry person can change, Bert Ghezzi outlines a successful strategy for using anger in the right way, based on scripture and his experiences as a leader in Christian groups. $2.95

Handling Conflict
Gerry Rauch

Down-to-earth advice on how to apply biblical wisdom to personal conflicts—on the job, at work, or at home. $3.95

Taming the Tongue
Mark Kinzer

Scriptural advice on how to control your speech, so that it builds up rather than tears down. Practical guidelines for handling gossip, negative humor, and slander. $2.95

Available at your Christian Bookstore or from:
**Servant Publications • Dept. 209 • P.O. Box 7455
Ann Arbor, Michigan 48107**
*Please include payment plus $.75 for postage.
Send for our FREE catalog of Christian
books, music, and cassettes.*